S0-AXY-957

The Canadian Revenue Stamp Catalogue 1991

by
E.S.J. van Dam

THE UNITRADE PRESS
TORONTO

COPYRIGHT NOTICE

The contents of this publication are owned exclusively by E.S.J. van Dam Ltd. and all rights thereto are reserved under the Pan-American and Universal Copyright conventions. No part of this publication may be reproduced, stored in a retrieval system, or transmitted in any form by any means, electronic or mechanical, including photocopying, without the prior written permission of E.S.J. van Dam Ltd.

Permission is hereby given for the use of index numbers, letters or symbols employed herein to magazines, periodicals and to stamp dealers in advertising matter or price lists prepared and issued for free distribution, provided the acknowledgement is given in every instance to the source, referring to this catalogue by the author's surname.

Permission is given for brief exerpts to be used for the reviewing of this publication in newspapers, magazines or periodicals provided the source of the material used is acknowledged.

Published by
THE UNITRADE PRESS
TORONTO

© 1990, 1986 E.S.J. van Dam Ltd.
ALL RIGHTS RESERVED

ISBN 0-919801-76-5

PRINTED AND BOUND IN CANADA

SUGGESTED RETAIL $10.95

THE UNITRADE PRESS

91 TYCOS DRIVE, TORONTO, ONTARIO,
CANADA M6B 1W3

TEL: (416) 787-5658
FAX: (416) 787-7104

PREFACE

This latest edition includes a record number of price changes, new listings and additions. Revenue stamps have become exceedingly popular and demand for better material far outstrips the available supply. In many cases only a few copies are known and yet the highest price for a revenue stamp is very modest compared to prices for postage stamps.

The engravings on revenue stamps are beyond compare, ranking with the most beautiful stamps in the world.

PRICES IN THIS CATALOGUE ARE FOR F/VF UNDAMAGED REVENUES (without creases or other faults) and are the current retail prices of E.S.J. van Dam Ltd.

The numbering system employed in this catalogue automatically identifies each stamp by province, type of issue and the stamp's individual number within the issue.

All prices shown in this catalogue are in Canadian dollars.

Prices are current retail prices for stamps in F/VF condition for the issue. VF stamps will sell at a premium, while lesser quality copies may sell for less.

Revenue stamps are usually punched, pen or crayon cancelled, punch perforated or have a combination of these cancellations as required by law.

Uncancelled revenues may occasionally have gum. Some were issued without gum.

This catalogue lists the basic issues and main varieties only. For more detailed listings please refer to the "ReveNews"© bulletins published by E.S.J. van Dam Ltd. These are available on a yearly subscription basis, sample available by sending $1 in cash or gummed, undamaged postage stamps to the address below.

Our thanks to the many friends and collectors who have taken the time to report new varieties, issues, etc. In particular, we would like to thank M.D. Bakker, Dr. Ian McTaggart Cowan, A. Koeppel, Wilmer C. Rockett, H.W. Lussey, D. Stickles, J.J. Gaudio, Chris Ryan and many others.

The author would very much like to hear from anyone with revenue items not listed in this catalogue.

Erling S.J. van Dam
P.O. Box 300
Bridgenorth, Ontario
Canada
K0L 1H0
Phone: (705) 292-7013
Fax: (705) 292-6311

CONTENTS

CANADA BILL STAMPS

1864 FIRST BILL ISSUE

Sheets of 100
Perf. 12½, 13½, 12½ x 13½, 13½ x 12½

FB1   FB10

FB15

			Uncan.	Used
FB1	1¢	blue	20.00	7.50
	a	horiz pair imperf vert.	—	1000.
	b	"." after "cent"	50.00	50.00
FB2	2¢	blue	12.50	6.00
FB3	3¢	blue	17.50	3.50
FB4	4¢	blue	10.00	4.00
FB5	5¢	blue	7.50	4.50
	a	vert. pair imperf horiz.	—	2000.
	b	G for C in Canada	200.00	200.00
FB6	6¢	blue	15.00	3.50
FB7	7¢	blue	6.50	5.50
	a	"SFVEN" error	300.00	300.00
FB8	8¢	blue	6.00	4.50
	a	"feather" in bun	100.00	100.00
FB9	9¢	blue	12.50	3.50
	a	vert. pr. impf. horiz	—	1,000
	b	"B" for "E" in NINE	200.00	200.00
FB10	10¢	blue	15.00	4.50
	a	1st a in Canada not joined	35.00	30.00
FB11	20¢	blue	20.00	6.00
	a	hor. pr. imperf. vert.	—	2500.
FB12	30¢	blue	60.00	30.00
	a	vert. pr. impf. between	—	2500.
FB13	40¢	blue	70.00	30.00
FB14	50¢	blue	75.00	30.00
FB15	$1	blue	250.00	85.00
FB16	$2	blue	25.00	25.00
FB17	$3	blue	25.00	25.00
	a	vert. pr. impf. horiz.	500.00	—
	b	"R" for "P" in STAMP	250.00	250.00
	c	initials in U.R. "$"	100.00	100.00

1865 SECOND BILL ISSUE

Sheets of 100, perf. 12, 13½

			Uncan.	Used
FB18	1¢	red	5.00	1.25
FB19	2¢	red	5.00	1.25
FB20	3¢	red	6.00	1.00
FB21	4¢	red	15.00	15.00
FB22	5¢	red	8.00	3.00
FB23	6¢	red	6.00	1.25
FB24	7¢	red	9.00	9.00

FB20

FB27

			Uncan.	Used
FB25	8¢	red	27.50	25.00
FB26	9¢	red	6.00	1.25
FB27	10¢	blue, perf 13½	10.00	2.00
	a	perf. 12	—	50.00
FB28	20¢	blue	12.50	3.50
FB29	30¢	blue	12.50	4.00
	a	imperf. pair	1000.	—
FB30	30¢	red	35.00	30.00
FB31	40¢	blue	35.00	25.00
	a	vert. pr. impf. horiz	1000.	—
FB32	50¢	blue, perf 13½	40.00	12.50
	a	imperf pair	1,000	—
	b	perf. 12	—	100.00

FB33

			Uncan.	Used
FB33	$1	red + green control	175.00	125.00
	a	vert. pr. impf. horiz.	1500.	—
FB34	$1	green + red control	150.00	100.00
FB35	$2	red + violet control	325.00	275.00
FB36	$3	red + blue control	300.00	275.00
	a	vert. pr. imperf horiz.	2000.	—
	b	imperf pair	3000.	—

1868 THIRD BILL ISSUE

Sheets of 100, perf 12, 11½ x 12

FB37

FB47

			Uncan.	Used
FB37	1¢	brown	1.00	0.50
	a	imperf single	—	250.00
FB38	2¢	brown	35.00	17.50
FB39	2¢	orange	1.00	0.50
	a	imperf between pair	—	1500.
FB40	3¢	green	1.00	0.30
	a	watermarked	—	300.00
	b	vert. pr. imperf horiz.	275.00	—
	c	imperf pair	100.00	—

				Uncan.	Used
FB40	d		double print	—	1,500
	e		imperf margin at right	35.00	35.00
FB41		4¢	brown	3.00	2.00
	a		imperf left or right	50.00	50.00
FB42		5¢	orange	1.50	0.70
	a		vert. pr. imperf horiz.	—	1500.
FB43		6¢	green	1.25	0.35
	a		watermarked	750.00	450.00
	b		hor. pr. imperf vert.	250.00	—
	c		FB43b watermarked	2000.	—
	d		re-entry left frame	100.00	100.00
FB44		7¢	orange	5.00	3.50
FB45		8¢	brown	5.00	4.00
FB46		9¢	green	2.50	0.50
FB47		10¢	blue	2.50	0.60
FB48		20¢	blue	4.50	0.75
	a		imperf at Left	35.00	35.00
FB49		30¢	blue	4.50	1.00
	a		imperf at Left	35.00	35.00
FB50		40¢	blue	7.50	3.50
FB51		50¢	blue	6.00	2.00

FB52   FB53a

FB52		$1	blue + black control	15.00	8.00
	a		imperf pair	95.00	—
FB53		$2	red + black control	25.00	20.00
	a		inverted ctr.	—	3500.
FB54		$3	green + black control	25.00	20.00

GAS INSPECTION
1875 CROWN
4½ mm red controls

FG1   FG3

FG1	25¢	blue	10.00	4.50
FG2	50¢	blue	12.50	5.00
FG3	$1	blue	12.50	7.50
FG4	$1.50	blue	15.00	4.00
FG5	$2	blue	12.50	3.50
FG6	$3	blue	120.00	95.00
FG7	$4	blue	160.00	145.00

			Uncan.	Used

1875 CROWN
3½ mm red controls

FG8   FG16

FG8	5¢	blue	250.00	250.00
FG9	25¢	blue	12.50	6.00
FG10	50¢	blue	15.00	3.50
FG11	$1	blue	20.00	6.00
FG12	$1.50	blue	750.00	700.00
FG13	$2	blue	400.00	350.00
FG14	$3	blue	20.00	5.00
FG15	$4	blue	20.00	17.50
FG16	$10	blue	25.00	8.00

1897 VICTORIA
Red control numbers

FG17   FG18   FG19

FG20   FG21   FG22

			Uncan.	Used
FG17	5¢	blue	750.00	675.00
FG18	25¢	blue	6.00	0.75
FG19	50¢	blue	5.00	0.75
FG20	60¢	blue	7.50	2.00
a		rouletted	—	3000.
FG21	75¢	blue	10.00	7.50
FG22	$1	blue	2.50	1.00
FG23	$1.50	blue	65.00	50.00
FG24	$2	blue	10.00	5.00

FG24   FG25   FG26

FG25	$4	blue	30.00	20.00
FG26	$10	blue	20.00	2.50

Blue or purple control numbers

FG27   FG28   FG29

FG27	$2	blue, blue control #	35.00	15.00
a		purple control #	25.00	4.50
FG28	$4	blue, purple #	20.00	2.50
a		off white paper	—	5.00
FG29	$10	blue, purple #	25.00	0.75

1915 GEORGE V

Red control numbers

FG30	$3	blue	25.00	20.00

Blue or purple control numbers

FG31	$3	blue	15.00	1.00
a		purple control #	20.00	2.50

FG30   FG31

ELECTRIC LIGHT INSPECTION
1895 CROWN
Blue control numbers

FE1   FE7

FE1	25¢	vermilion	20.00	12.50
FE2	50¢	vermilion	15.00	10.00
FE3	$1	vermilion	17.50	7.50
FE4	$2	vermilion	17.50	7.50
FE5	$3	vermilion	20.00	7.50
FE6	$5	vermilion	25.00	20.00
FE7	$10	vermilion	35.00	6.00

1900 ELECTRIC LIGHT EFFIGY

Blue or purple control numbers

FE8	25¢	vermilion, blue #	7.50	5.00
a	25¢	purple control #	7.50	5.00
b		thick paper, blue #	—	7.50
c		FE8a, imperf at right	—	35.00
FE9	25¢	carmine	14.50	9.50
FE10	50¢	vermilion	4.00	0.50
a		purple control #	4.00	0.50
FE11	60¢	vermilion, purple #	4.00	0.50
FE12	75¢	vermilion	4.00	1.50
a		purple control #	3.00	0.50
FE13	$1	vermilion	11.00	1.50
a		purple control #	11.00	1.50
FE14	$2	vermilion	15.00	1.00
a		purple control #	10.00	0.50

FE9

FE10

FE16

			Uncan.	Used
FE15	$3	vermilion	10.00	1.00
a		purple control #	20.00	2.00
b		jump # pair, purple #	—	10.00
FE16	$5	vermilion	8.50	1.00
a		purple control #	20.00	2.00
b		black control #	25.00	15.00
FE17	$10	vermilion	35.00	1.50
a		purple control #	35.00	1.00

ELECTRICITY & GAS INSPECTION
1930 GEORGE V
Blue control numbers

FEG1

FEG8

			Uncan.	Used
FEG1	50¢	vermilion	1.50	1.25
FEG2	60¢	vermilion	1.25	0.65
FEG3	75¢	vermilion	1.50	0.50
FEG4	$1	vermilion	5.50	5.50
FEG5	$2	vermilion	3.50	0.60
FEG6	$3	vermilion	4.00	0.45
FEG7	$10	vermilion	12.50	0.75
FEG8	60¢	blue	5.00	1.50
FEG9	$2	blue	4.00	0.75
FEG10	$3	blue	5.00	1.50
FEG11	$10	blue	15.00	0.90

WEIGHTS & MEASURES
1876 CROWN
4½ mm red numbers at top

FWM1

FWM5

FWM1	5¢	black	55.00	35.00
FWM2	10¢	black	55.00	35.00
FWM3	15¢	black	60.00	37.50
FWM4	20¢	black	65.00	35.00
FWM5	30¢	black	150.00	110.00

4½ mm red numbers at centre

FWM6   FWM9   FWM11

FWM6	1¢	blue	65.00	65.00
FWM7	2¢	blue	75.00	75.00
FWM8	30¢	black	120.00	110.00
FWM9	50¢	black	50.00	45.00
FWM10	$1	black	30.00	25.00

			Uncan.	Used
FWM11	$1.50	black	30.00	20.00
FWM12	$2	black	20.00	10.00

1878 CROWN
3½ mm red numbers at centre

FWM13	FWM14	FWM21

			Uncan.	Used
FWM13	1¢	black	30.00	25.00
FWM14	2¢	black	85.00	80.00
FWM15	5¢	black	40.00	20.00
FWM16	10¢	black	95.00	85.00
FWM17	15¢	black	125.00	110.00
FWM18	20¢	black	35.00	15.00
FWM19	30¢	black	35.00	20.00
FWM20	50¢	black	75.00	55.00
FWM21	$1	black	60.00	45.00

1887 CROWN
3½ mm, blue numbers at centre – sheets of 55

FWM22	FWM23	FWM33

FWM22	1¢	black	45.00	40.00
FWM23	2¢	black	25.00	20.00
FWM24	5¢	black	20.00	12.50
FWM25	10¢	black	17.50	12.50
FWM26	15¢	black	7.50	6.50
FWM27	20¢	black	10.00	4.00
FWM28	30¢	black	7.50	3.50
FWM29	50¢	black	7.50	3.50
FWM30	$1	black	10.00	5.00
FWM31	$1.50	black	10.00	3.50
FWM32	$2	black	12.50	3.00
FWM33		no value, red	25.00	—

1897 VICTORIA
Red control numbers

FWM34	FWM36	FWM38

			Uncan.	Used
FWM34	5¢	black	35.00	20.00
FWM35	10¢	black	110.00	95.00
FWM36	15¢	black	30.00	25.00
FWM37	20¢	black	20.00	15.00
FWM38	30¢	black	15.00	10.00
FWM39	50¢	black	7.50	3.50
FWM40	75¢	black	15.00	10.00

FWM41	FWM44

FWM41	$1	black	12.50	7.00
FWM42	$1.50	black	15.00	12.50
FWM43	$1.50	white label	20.00	10.00
FWM44	$2	black	15.00	10.00

Blue or purple control numbers

FWM46	FWM52

			Uncan.	Used
FWM45	5¢	black	50.00	35.00
a		purple control #	35.00	25.00
FWM46	10¢	black	20.00	17.50
a		purple control #	25.00	22.50
FWM47	15¢	black	20.00	15.00
a		purple control #	25.00	22.50
FWM48	30¢	black	10.00	7.50
a		purple control #	12.50	8.50
FWM49	50¢	black	75.00	65.00
FWM50	75¢	black	15.00	8.50
a		purple control #	15.00	7.50
FWM51	$1	black	7.50	6.00
a		purple control #	7.50	4.50
FWM52	$1.50	black	4.50	3.50
a		purple control #	4.50	3.50
b		jump # pair	—	25.00

1906 EDWARD VII
Red control numbers

FWM53

FWM56

FWM53	$5	black	35.00	25.00
FWM54	$10	black	35.00	15.00

Blue or purple control numbers

FWM55	$5	black	12.50	6.50
a	$5	purple control #	12.50	6.50
FWM56	$10	black	20.00	15.00
a		purple control #	15.00	7.00
b		jump # pair	—	15.00

1915 GEORGE V

FWM57

FWM58

FWM59

			Uncan.	Used
Red control numbers				
FWM57	$2	black	95.00	85.00
Blue or purple control numbers				
FWM58	20¢	black	10.00	5.00
a	20¢	purple control #	15.00	7.50
FWM59	$2	black	6.00	3.50
a	$2	purple control #	6.00	2.50
b		jump # pair	—	7.50

1930 GEORGE V
Blue control numbers

FWM60	5¢	black	7.50	7.50

FWM60

FWM67

FWM71

FWM61	10¢	black	3.50	3.50
FWM62	15¢	black	10.00	10.00
FWM63	20¢	black	5.00	5.00
FWM64	30¢	black	5.00	5.00
FWM65	50¢	black	2.00	1.50
FWM66	75¢	black	1.50	0.90
FWM67	$1	black	1.50	0.85
FWM68	$1.50	black	5.00	0.85
FWM69	$2	black	3.00	0.85
FWM70	$5	black	6.50	0.90
FWM71	$10	black	15.00	20.00

SUPREME COURT

1876 YOUNG QUEEN VICTORIA
Perf 12, 12 x 11½ + compound perf

Uncan. Used

FSC1 FSC5

FSC1	10¢	blue	95.00	75.00
FSC2	20¢	blue	85.00	65.00
FSC3	25¢	blue	95.00	85.00
FSC4	50¢	blue	95.00	70.00
FSC5	$1	blue	95.00	45.00
FSC6	$5	blue	85.00	30.00

1897 WIDOW QUEEN VICTORIA
Red control numbers

FSC7 FSC10

FSC7	10¢	blue	95.00	85.00
FSC8	$1	blue	95.00	35.00
FSC9	$5	blue	100.00	30.00
FSC10	$5	black	2000.	1200.

Uncan. Used

FSC11 FSC12

Purple control numbers

FSC11	$1	blue	120.00	100.00
FSC12	$5	black	750.00	550.00

1915 GEORGE V
Colour of control number in brackets

FSC15 FSC17

FSC13		10¢	blue (blue)	3500.	1000.
FSC14		10¢	rouletted (blue)	550.00	500.00
	a	10¢	rouletted (purple)	750.00	700.00
FSC15		25¢	blue (red)	700.00	350.00
FSC16		50¢	blue (purple)	500.00	250.00
FSC17		$1	blue (blue)	150.00	45.00

	Uncan.	Used

1935 GEORGE V - IN PROFILE
Sheets of 20

FSC18

FSC21   FSC22

1916 OVERPRINTED "IN PRIZE"

FSC19   FSC20

FSC18	$1	blue	30.00	6.00
FSC19	$30	on $1 horiz. bars	2000.	2000.
FSC20	$30	on $1 vertical bars	500.00	500.00
	a	black overprint	600.00	600.00

1938 GEORGE VI
Sheets of 20. Blue control numbers

FSC21	10¢	blue	11.00	8.00
FSC22	20	on 10¢	30.00	25.00
FSC23	25	on 10¢, silver o/p	475.00	450.00
FSC24	25¢	blue	15.00	12.50
FSC25	50¢	blue	20.00	20.00
FSC26	$5	blue	125.00	25.00

FSC30   FSC31

On 1876 issue				
FSC27	25¢	red + purple o/p	—	5,000
FSC28	50¢	red overprint	3750.	—
On 1897 issue				
FSC29	10¢	red overprint	500.00	500.00
	a	red + purple o/p	900.00	—
	b	double red o/p	2,000	—
FSC30	$1	red overprint	500.00	500.00
	a	double red overprint	2,000	—
	b	red & purple o/p	850.00	850.00
On 1915 issue				
FSC31	25¢	red overprint	950.00	900.00
	a	two red overprints	—	—

CUSTOMS DUTY
1912 CROWN
Comes in 2 sizes,
CA. 31½ & 32½ mm wide

	FCD1		FCD3	

			Uncan.	Used
FCD1	1¢	green	0.50	0.15
FCD2	2¢	carmine	0.75	0.15
FCD3	5¢	brown	2.00	0.45
FCD4	10¢	blue	2.50	0.50

1918 NIAGARA FALLS PROVISIONAL
Rubber Stamped "CUSTOMS DUTY"
on 1¢ orange War Tax

FCD5a

FCD5		o/p handstamped in black	—	600.00
	a	o/p stamped in violet	—	500.00

1935 Bilingual Customs Duty

	FCD6		FCD9	
FCD6	1¢	green	0.50	0.25
FCD7	2¢	orange	0.35	0.15
FCD8	5¢	brown	1.50	0.35
FCD9	10¢	blue	2.50	0.50

WAR TAX
FEBRUARY 12, 1915
Postage issue of 1912 overprinted "WAR TAX"

FWT1   FWT2

			Uncan.	Used
FWT1	5¢	blue	100.00	90.00
FWT2	20¢	olive	40.00	35.00
FWT3	50¢	black/brown	100.00	90.00

FEBRUARY 13, 1915
Postage issue of 1912
overprinted "INLAND REVENUE WAR TAX"

FWT4   FWT5

FWT4	5¢	blue	7.50	6.00
FWT5	20¢	olive	15.00	10.00
FWT6	50¢	black/brown	100.00	75.00

1915 GEORGE V

FWT7   FWT10a

FWT7	1¢	orange	0.25	0.15
	a	red "X" precancel	0.50	0.35
	b	black squares precan	—	300.00
	c	booklet pane of 6	475.00	—
	d	booklet with 4 panes	2,000	—
	e	"DIV. 17" precancel	—	350.00
FWT8	2¢	brown	0.75	0.10
	a	red "X" precancel	6.00	4.50
	b	black squares precan	—	350.00
	c	booklet pane of 6	5.00	25.00
	d	booklet with 2 panes	50.00	—
	e	booklet with 4 panes	30.00	—
	f	booklet with 8 panes	55.00	—
	g	major re-entry	—	50.00
	h	green binding on 8f	225.00	—
FWT9	3¢	green	3.00	0.15
	a	red "X" precancel	—	200.00
FWT10	4¢	blue	4.00	0.15

FWT11b   FWT11e

	a	red "X" precancel	60.00	50.00
FWT11	5¢	olive yellow	4.50	0.15
	a	red "X" precancel	7.50	5.50
	b	black squares precan	125.00	25.00
	c	FWT11b doubled	—	250.00
	d	flags precancel	—	100.00
	e	inverted flags prec	—	250.00

		Uncan.	Used

FWT12c   FWT15a

FWT12	8¢	brown	5.00	0.25
a		red "X" precancel	—	350.00
b		black squares precan	—	300.00
c		railway ties precan	—	250.00
FWT13	10¢	olive green	6.00	0.15
a		red "X" precancel	—	325.00
FWT14	13¢	vermilion	15.00	10.00
FWT15	25¢	carmine	7.50	0.25
a		railway ties precan	—	350.00
FWT16	50¢	brown	10.00	0.20

		Uncan.	Used

1915 COILS
Perf 8 horizontal

FWT17a   FWT18

FWT17	1¢	orange	—	45.00
a		"DIV 17" precancel	—	5.00
FWT18	2¢	brown	5.00	0.50
b		coil pair, perf. 12	15.00	10.00
a		perf 8 x 12	—	500.00
c		paste-up pair	45.00	10.00

1915 WINE STRIPS - ROULETTED

FWT19

FWT24

GEORGE V - HEAD UPRIGHT
Sheets of 20

FWT19	5¢	black	15.00	12.50
FWT20	10¢	black	30.00	25.00
FWT21	13¢	black	95.00	95.00
FWT22	25¢	black	30.00	25.00
FWT23	50¢	black	15.00	12.50

GEORGE V - HEAD SIDEWAYS

| FWT24 | 5¢ | black | 30.00 | 25.00 |
| FWT25 | 20¢ | black | 30.00 | 25.00 |

EXCISE TAX
1915-23 GEORGE V

FX1   FX2b

FX4   FX6a (Type I)

FX1	¼ ¢	Olive Green	0.35	0.35
a		red "X" precancel	—	350.00
b		flag precancel	—	100.00
FX2	½ ¢	carmine	0.35	0.35

a		red "X" precancel	—	100.00
b		flag precancel	—	35.00
c		flags inverted	—	150.00
d		1 flag inverted, 2 normal	—	500.00
e		normal & tripled flags	—	500.00
FX3	6¢	orange	2.00	0.10
FX4	7¢	brown	7.50	1.50
FX5	9¢	violet	8.00	1.50
FX6	15¢	orange	9.00	3.00
a	15¢	railway tie, type I	—	275.00

FX6b (Type II)   FX20

b	15¢	railway tie, type II	—	275.00
FX7	20¢	olive yellow	2.00	0.10
FX8	30¢	yellow brown	2.50	0.10
FX9	40¢	purple	3.50	0.15
FX10	60¢	blue	6.00	0.50

			Uncan.	Used
FX11	70¢	olive green	10.00	5.00
FX12	80¢	carmine	15.00	6.00
FX13	90¢	brown	15.00	5.00
FX14	$1	olive yellow	6.00	0.15
FX15	$2	green	15.00	0.25
FX16	$3	orange	20.00	2.00
FX17	$4	brown	45.00	5.00
FX18	$5	vermilion	25.00	1.50
a		orange	2,500	—
FX19	$10	orange	40.00	1.00
FX20	$100	green	150.00	25.00

OVERPRINTS ON 1915 EXCISE TAX

FX22

FX23

FX21	3⁄16 ¢	on 1⁄4 ¢	0.95	0.95
FX22	1⁄5 ¢	on 7¢	1.00	1.00
FX23	3⁄8 ¢	on 1⁄2 ¢, "CENT"	0.95	0.95
FX24	3⁄8 ¢	on 1⁄2 ¢, "Cent"	30.00	30.00
FX25	14	on 1⁄4 ¢	40.00	40.00

FX24

FX25

FX26

FX28

FX26	14	on 7¢, blue o/p	10.00	10.00
FX27	14	on 7¢, red overprint	10.00	10.00
a		diagonal overprint	25.00	—
b		pair 1 without o/p	75.00	—
c		overprint on back	50.00	—
d		o/p offset on back only	50.00	—
e		14 omitted	100.00	—
f		14 inverted, no Cents	100.00	—
g		overprint at top	35.00	—
h		4 Cents, 14 shifted o/p	25.00	—
FX28	14	on 9¢	12.50	12.50
a		inverted overprint	100.00	—
b		double overprint	35.00	—
c		diagonal overprint	50.00	—
d		pair, 1 without overprint	100.00	—
e		overprinted on back	50.00	—
f		"Cents" omitted	50.00	—
FX29	14	on 40¢	20.00	20.00
a		inverted overprint	100.00	—
b		o/p offset on back only	40.00	—
c		pair, 1 without overprint	125.00	—
d		o/p on back only	100.00	—
e		diagonal overprint	30.00	—

OVERPRINTS ON 1915 WAR TAX

Type A = CENT, Type B = Cent

FX30

FX31

FX33

			Uncan.	Used
FX30	3⁄4 ¢	on 1¢, type A	1.25	1.25
FX31	3⁄4 ¢	on 1¢, type B	2.50	2.50
a		thick overprint	10.00	10.00
FX32	1 1⁄2 ¢	on 1¢	2.75	2.75
FX33	2 1⁄4 ¢	on 3¢	25.00	15.00

TWO LEAF EXCISE TAX

1915-1928

FX34

FX36

FX42a

FX45

FX34	1⁄10 ¢	carmine	0.45	0.50
FX35	3⁄16 ¢	carmine	0.45	0.50
FX36	2¢	blue	0.75	0.10
a		booklet pane of 6	15.00	—
b		booklet with 2 panes	35.00	—
FX37	2 1⁄4 ¢	carmine	55.00	50.00
FX38	3¢	blue	0.75	0.10
a		booklet pane of 4	25.00	—
b		booklet with 2 panes	50.00	—
FX39	4¢	blue	2.50	0.10
FX40	6¢	blue	3.00	0.10
FX41	8¢	blue	4.50	0.10
FX42	10¢	blue	5.00	0.10
a		railway tie precancel	—	400.00
FX43	20¢	blue	7.50	0.15
FX44	50¢	blue	30.00	1.50
FX45	$100	green	150.00	20.00

Coils
Perf 8 Horizontal

FX46 (pair)

			Uncan.	Used
FX46	2¢	blue	2.50	0.50
a		coil pair	7.50	6.00
FX47	3¢	blue	5.00	3.00
a		coil pair	20.00	15.00
FX48	6¢	blue	75.00	35.00
a		coil pair	175.00	75.00

OVERPRINTS ON TWO LEAF EXCISE

FX49   FX50

FX49	3⁄20	on 1⁄10, o/p "CENT"	35.00	35.00
FX50	3⁄20	on 1⁄10, o/p "Cent"	35.00	35.00
a		light blue overprint	50.00	50.00
FX51	5¢	on 2¢	—	3500.

THREE LEAF EXCISE TAX
1934-48

FX52

FX61   FX82

FX52	3⁄20 ¢	red	0.35	0.35
FX53	3⁄16 ¢	red	0.40	0.40
FX54	1⁄5 ¢	red	0.50	0.50
FX55	9⁄40 ¢	red	3.00	3.00
FX56	1⁄4 ¢	red	0.25	0.25
FX57	1⁄4 ¢	green	0.25	0.15
FX58	3⁄10 ¢	red	2.50	2.50
FX59	3⁄8 ¢	red	1.75	1.75

			Uncan.	Used
FX60	1⁄2 ¢	red	0.25	0.15
FX61	1 ¢	blue	1.00	0.25
FX62	2 ¢	blue	0.75	0.10
FX63	21⁄4 ¢	red	20.00	15.00
FX64	3 ¢	blue	0.30	0.10
a		booklet pane of 4	25.00	—
b		booklet with 2 panes	55.00	—
FX65	4¢	blue	20.00	15.00
FX66	5¢	blue	3.50	0.25
FX67	6¢	blue	0.50	0.10
FX68	6¢	purple	0.30	0.15
FX69	8¢	blue	2.50	0.75
FX70	8¢	red	95.00	85.00
FX71	10¢	blue	2.50	0.15
FX72	12¢	blue	60.00	50.00
FX73	13¢	blue	175.00	160.00
FX74	14¢	blue	20.00	15.00
FX75	15¢	blue	20.00	15.00
FX76	20¢	blue	2.25	0.20
FX77	20¢	red	15.00	10.00
FX78	25¢	blue	4.50	0.30
FX79	30¢	blue	10.00	1.75
FX80	50¢	blue	10.00	0.30
FX81	70¢	blue	25.00	20.00
FX82	$1	violet	20.00	5.00
FX83	$1	green	10.00	0.25
FX84	$1	red	10.00	0.75
FX85	$2	green	17.50	0.75
FX86	$2	red	20.00	16.00
FX87	$3	green	22.50	5.50
FX88	$4	green	17.50	12.50
FX89	$5	green	17.50	1.25
FX90	$5	red	17.50	6.00
FX91	$10	green	30.00	1.50
FX92	$10	red	30.00	3.00
FX93	$25	green	60.00	5.50
FX94	$100	green	150.00	17.50

COILS
Perf 11 Horizontal

FX95	2¢	blue	10.00	7.50

FX95

a		coil pair	25.00	20.00
b		paste-up pair	35.00	—
FX96	3¢	blue	3.50	2.00
a		coil pair	8.75	5.00
b		paste-up pair	25.00	—
FX97	6¢	blue	7.50	7.50
a		coil pair	20.00	17.50
b		paste-up pair	30.00	—

IMPERFORATED THREE LEAF EXCISE TAX
Issued without gum

FX98   FX102

			Uncan.	Used
FX98	2¢	blue	2.00	0.25
FX99	5¢	blue	2.50	0.25
FX100	6¢	blue	100.00	6.00
FX101	8¢	blue	3.50	1.00
FX102	8¢	red	85.00	75.00

OVERPRINTS ON THREE LEAF EXCISE TAX

FX103

FX116

FX114

FX135

FX103	1/5	on 3/20 ¢ red	5.00	5.00
FX104	1/5	on 1/4 ¢ green	4.00	4.00
FX105	3/10	on 9/40 ¢ red	4.00	4.00
a		"31/10" variety	35.00	35.00
FX106	2/5	on 3/16 ¢ red	9.00	9.00
FX107	1/2	on 3/20	4.50	4.50
FX108	1/2	on 3/16	4.50	4.50
FX109	1/2	on 3/10	4.50	4.50
FX110	1/2	on 9/40	4.50	4.50
FX111		1/2 on 3/8	5.00	5.00
FX112	5	on 2, inverted o/p	—	375.00
FX113	14	on 3/16	15.00	15.00
FX114	14	on 1/4 ¢	4.00	4.00
FX115	14	on 1¢	90.00	85.00
FX116	14	on 15¢	10.00	10.00
FX117	14	on 25¢	10.00	10.00
FX118	14	on 50¢	25.00	25.00
FX119	14	on 70¢	10.00	10.00
a		inverted o/p	60.00	—
b		normal & inverted	100.00	—
c		FX119b doubled	100.00	—
d		diagonal o/p	100.00	—
e		pair 1 without o/p	100.00	—
f		doubled + invert tripled	100.00	—
FX120	14	on $2, blue o/p	20.00	20.00
FX121	14	on $2, red o/p	8.00	8.00
a		diagonal o/p	35.00	—
FX122	14	on $3, blue o/p	15.00	15.00
a		inverted o/p	50.00	—
b		pair 1 without o/p	125.00	—
FX123	14	on $3, red o/p	12.50	12.50
FX124	14	on $4, blue o/p	12.50	12.50
FX125	14	on $4, red overprint	10.00	10.00
a		double overprint	75.00	—
b		diagonal overprint	75.00	—
FX126	14	on $5, red overprint	25.00	25.00
a		diagonal overprint	75.00	—
FX127	15	on 2¢, black o/p	75.00	15.00
FX128	15	on 2¢, blue o/p	—	60.00
FX129	20	on 15¢ blue	60.00	27.50
FX130	24	on 15¢ blue	25.00	20.00
FX131	28	on 1/2 ¢ red	75.00	75.00
FX132	28	on 21/4 ¢ red	30.00	30.00

			Uncan.	Used
FX133	28	on 12¢, blue o/p	75.00	65.00
FX134	28	on 12¢, red o/p	12.50	12.50
FX135	28	on 20¢ red	15.00	15.00

OVERPRINTS ON IMPERFORATES
Issued without gum

FX136

FX137

FX140

FX136	5	on 2¢ blue	—	20.00
FX137	8	on 5¢ blue	6.00	5.00
FX138	8	on 6¢, blue o/p	17.50	4.00
FX139	8	on 6¢, purple o/p	17.50	4.50
FX140	8	on 6¢, light red o/p	150.00	125.00
a		dark red overprint	200.00	—

WAR SAVINGS STAMPS
1918
English inscription

FWS1	25¢	orange	45.00	—
FWS2	$5	green	500.00	500.00

French inscription

FWS1

FWS2

FWS3	25¢	orange	2500.	—
FWS4	$5	green	—	—

FWS3

1940-41

			Uncan.	Used
FWS5	25¢	blue, yellow gum	5.00	—
	a	blue, white gum	15.00	—
	b	pane of 8, yellow gum	65.00	—
	c	pane of 8, white gum	200.00	—
	d	booklet with 2xFWS5C	400.00	—

FWS5   FWS6

			Uncan.	Used
FWS5	e	book with 5xFWS5b	375.00	—
	f	book with 10xFWS5b	750.00	—
	g	book with 25 panes	—	—
FWS6	25¢	carmine, spitfire	25.00	—
	a	booklet pane of 8	250.00	—
	b	booklet with 5 panes	1250.	—
FWS7	25¢	carmine, ships	6.00	—
FWS8	25¢	carmine, pilots	6.00	—
FWS9	25¢	carmine, destroyer	6.00	—
FWS10	25¢	carmine, tank	6.00	—
FWS11	25¢	carmine, bomber	6.00	—
FWS12	25¢	carmine, nurses	6.00	—
FWS13	25¢	carmine, soldier	6.00	—
FWS14	25¢	carmine, A.A. gun	6.00	—
FWS15	pane	8 diff FWS7/14	65.00	—
	a	booklet with 5 panes	350.00	—
	b	Book with 4 line inscrip.	400.00	—

FWS15

EMBOSSED CHEQUE STAMPS

1915-53

			Uncan.	Used
FCH1	2¢	red, small "A A"	3.50	0.35
	a	on complete cheque	10.00	2.50
FCH2		rectangular embossed	35.00	35.00
	a	on complete cheque	—	150.00

FCH1   FCH2

CONSULAR FEE STAMPS

1949

FCF2   FCF3

FCF1	25¢ blue	375.00	300.00
FCF2	50¢ carmine	80.00	60.00
FCF3	$1 orange	65.00	50.00
FCF4	$2 brown	65.00	50.00
FCF5	$5 green	225.00	200.00

FCH3   FCH5

FCH3	3¢	red, no letters	40.00	30.00
FCH4	6¢	red, no letters	75.00	30.00
FCH5	3¢	red, small "C C"	6.00	3.50
	a	on complete cheque	25.00	17.50
FCH6	6¢	red, small "C C"	7.00	4.00

MEDICINE STAMPS
1909-1919

FM1   FM2

			Uncan.	Used
FM1		1909 red, perf 12	0.35	—
FM2		1919 black, perf 12	2.50	—

PLAYING CARD STAMP
1947

FPC1

FPC1		violet p. 11 x imprf	3.50	3.00
	a	coil pair	150.00	—

Various different playing card precancels exist.

POSTAL NOTE & SCRIP STAMPS
1932-48 FIRST ISSUE - LARGE SIZE
FPS15,18,19,21,22 inscribed "Postal Scrip"; rest "Postal Note"

FPS1   FPS12

FPS20

FPS1	1¢	blue	0.75	0.75
	a	booklet pane of 100	85.00	—
	b	book with 5 x FPS1a	425.00	—
FPS2	1¢	brown	0.45	0.45
FPS3	2¢	blue	1.75	1.75
FPS4	2¢	olive	0.45	0.45
FPS5	3¢	blue	0.40	0.40
FPS6	4¢	blue	0.45	0.45
	a	imperf between pair	500.00	—
FPS7	5¢	blue	0.50	0.50
	a	pane of 25	500.00	—
	b	book with 8 panes	5000.	—

			Uncan.	Used
FPS8	6¢	blue	0.55	0.55
FPS9	7¢	blue	0.60	0.60
FPS10	8¢	blue	0.75	0.75
FPS11	9¢	blue	1.25	1.25
FPS12	10¢	black	0.75	0.75
FPS13	20¢	green	3.75	3.75
FPS14	25¢	orange	1.75	1.75
FPS15	30¢	blue	3.75	2.75
FPS16	40¢	purple	4.00	3.00
FPS17	50¢	brown	4.00	3.00
FPS18	60¢	yellow	4.50	3.50
FPS19	70¢	red	4.50	4.00
FPS20	75¢	purple	35.00	30.00
FPS21	80¢	green	5.50	5.00
FPS22	90¢	brown	5.75	5.25

1967 POSTAL SCRIP - SECOND ISSUE
Approx. 20½ x 17 mm

FPS33   FPS38

FPS23	1¢	brown	2.50	2.25
FPS24	2¢	green	2.50	2.25
FPS25	3¢	purple	4.50	4.00
FPS26	4¢	pink	2.50	2.25
FPS27	5¢	blue	4.50	4.00
FPS28	6¢	olive	7.50	6.00
FPS29	7¢	orange	6.00	5.00
FPS30	8¢	blue	7.50	6.00
FPS31	9¢	reddish purple	5.00	4.50
FPS32	10¢	slate green	7.50	6.50
FPS33	20¢	green	10.00	10.00
FPS34	30¢	blue	7.50	6.00
FPS35	40¢	olive	4.50	4.25
FPS36	50¢	brown	5.00	4.75
FPS37	60¢	yellow	8.50	8.50
FPS38	70¢	red	5.25	5.00
FPS39	80¢	green	6.00	5.00
FPS40	90¢	brown	8.50	7.50
	a	cello pack	125.00	—

THIRD ISSUE - NEW SMALLER SIZE
Approx. 20 x 16 mm

FPS42

FPS49   FPS58

FPS41	1¢	does not exist	—	—
FPS42	2¢	green	10.00	10.00
FPS43	3¢	purple	10.00	10.00

			Uncan.	Used
FPS44	4¢	pink	10.00	10.00
FPS45	5¢	blue	10.00	10.00
FPS46	6¢	olive	10.00	10.00
FPS47	7¢	orange	10.00	10.00
FPS48	8¢	blue	10.00	10.00
FPS49	9¢	reddish purple	10.00	10.00
FPS50	10¢	slate green	10.00	10.00
FPS51	20¢	green	20.00	20.00
FPS52	30¢	blue	15.00	15.00
FPS53	40¢	olive	15.00	15.00
FPS54	50¢	brown	20.00	20.00
FPS55	60¢	yellow	20.00	20.00
FPS56	70¢	red	20.00	20.00
FPS57	80¢	green	20.00	20.00
FPS58	90¢	brown	25.00	25.00
a		cello pack	250.00	—
b		stapled cello pack	250.00	—

UNEMPLOYMENT INSURANCE STAMPS

These stamps are found in three different ways. Mint usually with gum, used, and specimens. Specimens are overprinted "CANCELLED" or "SPECIMEN," some also having a small round punch-hole. Some values have only been seen as specimens. Items not priced have not been seen.

1941 ISSUE.
Denomination in circular panel

FU1

			Uncan.	Used	Spec.
FU1	24¢	slate green	15.00	15.00	15.00
FU2	27¢	red brown	15.00	5.00	15.00
FU3	33¢	rose	15.00	10.00	15.00
FU4	40¢	bistre	15.00	10.00	15.00
FU5	43¢	light blue	15.00	10.00	15.00
FU6	46¢	mauve	4.50	2.50	5.00
FU7	51¢	green	5.00	2.50	5.00
FU8	57¢	orange	3.50	2.75	5.00

FU10

FU9	63¢	bistre brown	2.50	1.25	5.00
FU10	$1	violet	45.00	35.00	35.00
FU11	$1.11	green	35.00	35.00	35.00
FU12	$1.24	orange	35.00	35.00	35.00
FU13	$1.37	brown	35.00	35.00	35.00

		Uncan.	Used	Spec.

1948 ISSUE
Denomination in rectangular panel

FU15

FU14	18¢	red brown	25.00	20.00	7.50
	a	OHMS perfin	—	—	250.00
FU15	30¢	rose	9.00	7.50	5.00
FU16	39¢	bistre	20.00	15.00	10.00
FU17	42¢	light blue	17.50	12.50	6.00
FU18	45¢	mauve	12.00	7.50	6.00
FU19	48¢	green	7.50	6.00	5.00
FU20	60¢	vermilion	7.50	6.00	5.00
FU21	72¢	bistre brown	3.50	2.50	5.00
	a	red CANCELLED	—	—	20.00
FU22	84¢	blue	18.00	15.00	10.00
FU23	84¢	yellow	12.50	10.00	—
FU24	$1.04	green	15.00	12.50	30.00
	a	OHMS perfin	—	—	395.00
FU25	$1.30	vermilion	7.50	1.75	5.00

FU24

FU26	$1.56	brown	45.00	40.00	9.00
	a	red CANCELLED	—	—	15.00
FU27	$1.82	blue	25.00	20.00	17.50

1950 Issue
No class number above panel

FU28

FU35

FU28	36¢	bistre	15.00	10.00	6.00
FU29	48¢	green	2.00	1.50	5.00
FU30	60¢	vermilion	3.00	1.50	5.00
FU31	72¢	brown	3.50	1.75	10.00
FU32	84¢	yellow	3.75	2.75	5.00

			Uncan.	Used	Spec.
FU33	96¢	blue	3.50	1.75	7.50
FU34	$1.08	rose	3.50	1.75	7.50
FU35	$1.56	bistre	45.00	40.00	25.00
FU36	$1.82	yellow	45.00	40.00	25.00
FU37	$2.08	blue	20.00	20.00	20.00
FU38	$2.34	rose	8.50	6.50	7.50

1955 Issue

	FU39			FU40	
FU39	32¢	brown	2.50	1.50	5.00
FU40	48¢	green	2.50	1.25	5.00
FU41	60¢	vermilion	2.50	1.25	6.00
FU42	72¢	bistre brwn	2.50	1.25	5.00
FU43	84¢	yellow	2.75	1.50	5.00
FU44	96¢	blue	3.00	1.75	5.00
FU45	$1.04	mauve	4.00	1.50	5.00
FU46	$1.12	slate blue	4.50	1.50	5.00
FU47	$1.20	yellow grn	4.75	1.25	5.00
FU48	$1.30	orange	9.50	5.00	7.50

	FU48				
FU49	$1.56	brown	5.50	2.25	6.00
FU50	$1.82	yellow	5.50	2.25	6.00
FU51	$2.08	blue	6.00	3.00	6.50
FU52	$2.26	mauve	6.75	2.50	7.50
FU53	$2.42	slate	7.50	3.50	7.50
FU54	$2.60	yellow grn	15.00	5.00	8.50
FU55	$2.60	emerald	15.00	3.50	7.50

1957 FISHERMAN ISSUE
Fisherman stamps were used by Canada's professional fishermen. Mint copies and actual used copies are rare.

	FU56			FU57	
FU56	32¢	brown	50.00	20.00	25.00
FU57	48¢	green	50.00	20.00	25.00
FU58	60¢	vermilion	50.00	20.00	25.00
FU59	72¢	brown	50.00	20.00	25.00
FU60	84¢	yellow	50.00	20.00	25.00
FU61	96¢	blue	50.00	20.00	25.00
FU62	$1.04	mauve	50.00	20.00	25.00

			Uncan.	Used	Spec.
FU63	$1.12	slate	50.00	20.00	25.00
FU64	$1.20	yellow grn	50.00	20.00	25.00

1958 FISHERMAN ISSUE
New Design

	FU65			FU66	
FU65	32¢	brown	50.00	30.00	25.00
FU66	48¢	green	50.00	30.00	25.00
FU67	60¢	vermilion	50.00	20.00	25.00
FU68	72¢	brown	50.00	30.00	25.00
FU69	84¢	yellow	50.00	10.00	25.00
FU70	96¢	blue	50.00	30.00	25.00
FU71	$1.04	mauve	50.00	30.00	25.00
FU72	$1.12	slate	50.00	30.00	25.00
FU73	$1.20	yellow grn	50.00	20.00	25.00
a	light doubling of "$1.20"		—	20.00	50.00

1960 ISSUE

	FU74			FU75	
FU74	40¢	brown	2.75	2.50	5.00
FU75	76¢	green	2.75	1.75	5.00
FU76	92¢	brown	3.00	2.00	5.00
FU77	$1.08	orange	3.25	1.25	5.00
FU78	$1.32	bistre	4.00	1.75	5.00

	FU78				

	FU80			FU83	
FU79	$1.44	rose	4.00	1.75	7.50
FU80	$1.56	blue	4.50	2.00	7.50
FU81	$1.72	mauve	5.00	2.00	6.00

			Uncan.	Used	Spec.
FU82	$1.88	slate blue	5.50	2.25	6.00
FU83	$3.12	grey	45.00	45.00	45.00
FU84	$3.38	blue	10.00	10.00	10.00
FU85	$3.72	olive grey	10.00	7.50	10.00
FU86	$4.08	coral	8.00	7.50	10.00

1960 Fisherman Issue

FU87   FU95

FU87	40¢	brown	35.00	25.00	25.00
FU88	76¢	green	35.00	20.00	25.00
FU89	92¢	brown	35.00	20.00	25.00
FU90	$1.08	yellow	35.00	20.00	25.00
FU91	$1.32	bistre	35.00	20.00	25.00
FU92	$1.44	rose	35.00	20.00	25.00
FU93	$1.56	blue	35.00	20.00	25.00
FU94	$1.72	mauve	35.00	20.00	25.00
FU95	$1.88	slate	35.00	20.00	25.00

FU105

			Uncan.	Used	Spec.
FU96	40¢	rose	15.00	6.00	25.00
FU97	70¢	bistre	15.00	6.00	25.00
FU98	$1	brown	15.00	6.00	25.00
FU99	$1.30	grey	15.00	6.00	25.00
FU100	$1.60	purple	20.00	6.00	25.00
FU101	$1.90	dull green	20.00	6.00	25.00
FU102	$2.20	olive grn	20.00	7.50	25.00
FU103	$2.50	orange	25.00	10.00	25.00
FU104	$2.80	light green	20.00	7.50	25.00
FU105	$3.12	brown	75.00	75.00	75.00

1968 Fisherman Issue

FU106   FU114

FU106	40¢	rose	—	—	25.00
FU107	70¢	bistre	—	—	25.00
FU108	$1	brown	—	—	25.00
FU109	$1.30	grey	—	—	25.00
FU110	$1.60	purple	—	—	25.00
FU111	$1.90	slate	—	—	25.00
FU112	$2.20	olive green	—	—	25.00
FU113	$2.50	orange	—	—	25.00
FU114	$2.80	light green	—	—	25.00

1968 Issue
Similar to 1960 Issue, but with new values and colours

FU96   FU97

LOCK SEALS
For use on Locks of Excise Warehouses and Distilleries

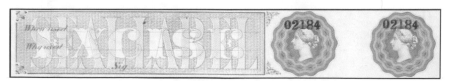

FLS2

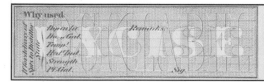  

FLS7

			Uncan.	Used				Uncan.	Used
FLS1		black and red	350.00	350.00		a	booklet pane of 2	750.00	—
FLS2		blue, Victoria	35.00	35.00	FLS5		blue, Coat of Arms	375.00	375.00
	a	booklet pane of 2	75.00	75.00	FLS6		blue, no controls	375.00	375.00
	b	horiz. lines only	100.00	100.00	FLS7		red, Victoria	150.00	150.00
FLS3		blue, Edward VII	375.00	375.00		a	booklet pane of 2	300.00	300.00
	a	booklet pane of 2	750.00	—		b	horiz. lines only	300.00	300.00
FLS4		blue, George V	375.00	375.00	FLS8		red, Edward VII	375.00	375.00

PETROLEUM LABELS 1886
For use on petroleum containers

FLP1

FLP5

FPL1		blue, imperf	75.00	75.00
FPL2		blue, rouletted	75.00	75.00
FPL3		light blue, p.12½	75.00	75.00
	a	dark blue, p.12½	75.00	75.00
FPL4		blue, perf. 14	75.00	75.00
FPL5		vermilion, imperf	75.00	75.00
FPL6		vermilion, rouletted	75.00	75.00
FPL7		vermilion, p. 12½	75.00	75.00
FPL8		vermilion, perf 14	75.00	75.00

ONE LINE INSCRIPTION AT TOP ONLY:
"This label must be destroyed when can is empty . . ."

FPL9	blue, perf. 12½	150.00	150.00
FPL10	carmine, p. 12½	225.00	225.00

WILDLIFE HABITAT CONSERVATION

Used on hunting licenses. All years except 1985 issued in booklet of 1 and sheets of 16

FWH1

FWH1	$4	1985 Mallards	15.00	15.00
	a	on license	—	15.00
FWH2	$4	1986 Canvasbacks	15.00	15.00
	a	on license	—	15.00
	b	sheet of 16	250.00	—
	c	plate block of 4	75.00	—
FWH3	6.50	1987 Canada Geese	11.50	10.00
	a	on license	—	12.50
	b	Cpl. sheet of 16	250.00	—
	c	plate block of 4	75.00	—
FWH4	6.50	multicolour Pintails	11.00	—
	a	on license	—	12.50
	b	sheet of 16	175.00	—
	c	plate block of 4	50.00	—
FWH5	7.50	1989 Snow Geese	11.00	—
	a	on license	—	12.50
	b	sheet of 16	175.00	—
	c	plate block of 4	50.00	—

PROVINCE OF ALBERTA

	Uncan.	Used

LAW STAMPS
1906-07 Scroll Background.
Overprint color in ( )

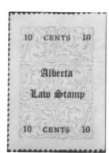 

	AL2		Uncan.	Used
		AL16		
AL1	10¢	purple	35.00	20.00
a		doubled background	—	100.00
AL2	10¢	yellow	35.00	10.00
a		doubled background	—	100.00
AL3	10¢	red (green)	20.00	6.00
a		doubled background	—	100.00
AL4	10¢	red (black)	20.00	6.00
a	10¢	brown	30.00	10.00
b		doubled background	—	100.00
AL5	20¢	red	100.00	85.00
a		doubled background	—	200.00
AL6	25¢	red (black)	30.00	6.00
a		pinperforated	—	35.00
b		"2.5" variety	—	25.00
AL7	25¢	red (green)	35.00	6.00
a		"2.5" variety	—	25.00
b		doubled background	—	100.00
AL8	25¢	yellow	30.00	8.00
a		pinperforated	—	25.00
b		doubled background	—	100.00
c		"2.5" variety	—	25.00
AL9	25¢	purple	125.00	85.00
a		doubled background	—	200.00
AL10	25¢	green	85.00	75.00
a		"2.5" variety	—	125.00
AL11	25¢	grey	600.00	325.00
AL12	50¢	green	30.00	7.50
a		major p/p shift	—	—
AL13	50¢	red	30.00	6.00
AL14	75¢	red	30.00	6.00
a		doubled background	—	100.00
AL15	$1	red	35.00	6.50
a		doubled background	—	100.00
b		imperf between pair	—	500.00
AL16	$1	brown, "ONE DOLLAR"	50.00	8.50
a		doubled background	—	100.00
b		major o/p shift	—	—

1907-10

Justice Standing

AL17	5¢	grey	10.00	9.00
a	5¢	brown grey	12.50	10.00
AL18	10¢	orange	1.50	0.60
AL19	20¢	chestnut	12.50	3.00
AL20	25¢	red	3.50	1.00
AL21	50¢	green	5.50	1.00

	AL17		Uncan.	Used
		AL23		
AL22	75¢	violet	15.00	1.00
a	75¢	blue	—	75.00
AL23	$1	dark blue	12.50	1.00
AL24	$2	lake	25.00	2.50
AL25	$3	greenish black	20.00	3.50
AL26	$5	yellow ochre	50.00	7.50
a		imperf between pair	—	500.00

1910-30

Justice Seated

	AL28			
		AL38		
AL27	5¢	pale brown	6.00	5.00
AL28	10¢	olive green	2.50	1.50
AL29	20¢	brown violet	5.00	4.00
AL30	25¢	lake red	2.00	0.50
a	25¢	carmine	2.50	0.75
AL31	50¢	green	2.75	0.50
AL32	75¢	violet	3.50	2.00
AL33	$1	blue	5.00	0.50
AL34	$2	grey	6.50	3.00
AL35	$3	brown	15.00	7.50
AL36	$3	red brown	250.00	250.00
AL37	$5	black	35.00	20.00
AL38	$5	yellow orange	200.00	200.00
AL39	$10	sepia	35.00	20.00

PROSPERITY CERTIFICATE
1936

		AP1		
AP1	1¢	green	10.00	—
a		on certificate	—	75.00

Uncan.   Used

Uncan.   Used

ALBERTA TELEPHONE FRANKS
Issued without gum

	AT1		AT3		AT6		
AT1	5¢	orange, series A			—	20.00
	a	watermarked			—	30.00
	b	complete pane of 20			—	425.00
AT2	25¢	grey, series A			—	25.00
	a	watermarked			—	35.00
	b	complete pane of 20			—	500.00
AT3	5¢	red, series B			—	750.00
AT4	25¢	mauve, series B			—	750.00
AT5	5¢	orange, 1909			—	750.00
AT6	25¢	grey, 1909			—	750.00

VACATION PAY STAMPS
1953 First issue
Board of Industrial Relations
Used copies multiple punch

	AV3		AV6		
AV1	1¢	light green	10.00	8.00
AV2	2¢	green	10.00	8.00
AV3	5¢	pale blue	10.00	8.00
AV4	10¢	orange	10.00	8.00
AV5	25¢	yellow	15.00	10.00
AV6	50¢	carmine	15.00	12.50
AV7	$1	pink	20.00	15.00
AV8	$2	olive bistre	30.00	25.00

1955 Second Issue
Value in each corner
Used copies multiple punch

AV9

AV9	1¢	brown	7.50	7.00
AV10	2¢	green	10.00	9.00
AV11	5¢	grey blue	10.00	9.00
AV12	10¢	orange	11.00	9.00
AV13	25¢	yellow	12.50	10.00

AV15

AV14	50¢	red	17.50	15.00
AV15	$1	purple	20.00	15.00
AV16	$2	olive	25.00	20.00

Third Issue
Value in lower corners only
Used copies multiple punch

AV17

AV17	1¢	brown	7.50	7.00
	a	1¢	ochre	7.50	7.00
AV18	2¢	green	7.50	7.00
	a	2¢	yellow green	7.50	7.00

AV20a

AV19	5¢	blue	10.00	8.00
AV20	10¢	yellow orange	10.00	8.00
	a	10¢	orange red	10.00	8.00
AV21	25¢	lake brown	12.50	10.00
AV22	50¢	red	15.00	12.50
AV23	$1	purple	18.00	15.00
AV24	$2	olive	25.00	20.00

See page 70 for complete listing of Alberta hunting stamps.

PROVINCE OF BRITISH COLUMBIA

Uncan. Used   Uncan. Used

LAW STAMPS
1879-80 First series

	BCL2			
BCL1	10¢	blue	8.00	3.00
BCL2	30¢	blue	10.00	4.00
BCL3	50¢	blue	10.00	5.00
BCL4	$1	blue	25.00	15.00

1888-91 Second series
Engraved. Perf. 11
30c & 50c "LAW STAMP" in white; 10c diagonal shading only in cloak, white justice.

	BCL5		BCL6	
BCL5	10¢	black	10.00	7.50
a		watermarked	100.00	100.00
b		perf 11 x 5-1/2	175.00	175.00
c		hor.pr. imperf between	—	600.00
BCL6	30¢	vermilion	17.50	15.00
a		watermarked	100.00	100.00
b		imperf single	—	200.00
BCL7	50¢	brown	17.50	12.50
a		watermarked	100.00	100.00
BCL8	10¢	carbon black	10.00	7.50
a		bisect on document	—	200.00

1893-1901 Third series
Lithographed. Perf. 11, 12
"RI" of BRITISH joined, left leg comes to point, cross hatched shading in cloak.

BCL9	10¢	slate grey	7.50	1.00
BCL10	30¢	orange, perf. 11	25.00	15.00

	BCL11		BCL12	
BCL11	50¢	buff, perf. 11	25.00	10.00
a		bisect on document	—	250.00

BCL12-15 broken "S" in British

BCL12	10¢	black	7.50	1.00
a		pinperf	25.00	10.00
b		hor. pr. imperf between	—	500.00
c		single imperf horiz.	—	100.00
BCL13	30¢	rose	30.00	10.00
a		pinperf	—	17.50
BCL14	50¢	brown	20.00	5.00
a		pinperf	30.00	10.00
BCL15	$1	blue	40.00	35.00
a		pinperf	50.00	45.00

1905-12 Fourth Series
Lithographed. Perf. 12
Right leg of "R" in BRITISH curled up and not joined to the "I".

	BCL17		BCL21	
BCL16	10¢	black	6.00	1.25
a		pinperf	50.00	45.00
b		bisect on document	—	275.00
c		double print	—	1,500
d		hor. pr. impf. vert.	—	600.00
BCL17	25¢	green	25.00	7.50
BCL18	30¢	orange	45.00	15.00
a		pinperf	—	30.00
BCL19	30¢	rose	45.00	15.00
a		vert. pair. impf. horiz	—	500.00
BCL20	50¢	brown	10.00	1.00
a		yellow brown	15.00	5.00
b		pinperf	—	17.50
BCL21	$1	blue	12.50	2.50
a		pinperf	150.00	30.00
b		imperf pair	—	500.00

1912-26 Fifth Series

"R" of BRITISH straight right leg. Hairy legs on justice

			Uncan.	Used
	BCL24		BCL27	
BCL22	10¢	black	3.50	0.50
a		hor. pair impf. between	—	550.00
b		perf x roulette	—	35.00
c		pinperf	—	50.00
d		BCL22 + inverted BCL26	—	1500.
e		double print	—	—
f		BCL22 + BCL26 at top	—	1250.
BCL23	25¢	green	3.00	0.50
a		hor. pair impf. btwn	500.00	—
b		vert. pr. imperf btwn	500.00	—
c		pinperf	—	25.00
BCL24	30¢	orange	15.00	15.00
a		pinperf	—	25.00
BCL25	50¢	brown	10.00	0.50
a		perf x roulette	—	35.00
b		bisect on document	—	125.00
c		BCL25+BCL22 invert on top	—	1250.
d		pinperf	—	50.00
BCL26	$1	blue	15.00	1.00
a		perf x roulette	—	35.00
b		pinperf	—	35.00
c		double print	—	150.00
d		bisect on document	—	250.00
e		imperf pair	—	—
f		BCL26 normal+BCL22 inv.	—	—
BCL27	$5	crimson	35.00	10.00
a		strip of 3 impf vert	750.00	—
b		pinperf	—	100.00

1928-32 Sixth Series

Shadow of left foot extends to edge of pedestal.

	BCL30		BCL31	
BCL28	10¢	black	5.00	2.50
a		double print	—	200.00
BCL29	30¢	orange	15.00	15.00

			Uncan.	Used
BCL30	50¢	brown	2.50	1.50
BCL31	$1	blue	15.00	1.75

1933-41 Seventh Series

The shadow of left foot does not extend to edge of pedestal.

10¢	Die I	Solid panels around "10"
	Die II	Broken panels around "10"
50¢	Die I	Two vertical lines left of "50"
	Die II	One vertical line left of "50"
$1	Die I	"S" similar to BCL31
	Die II	"S" in leaning position
	Die III	"R" in DOLLAR curved at tip

	BCL32		BCL35	
BCL32	10¢	grey, die I	10.00	6.00
a		die II	5.00	0.50
b		pinperf	—	25.00
BCL33	30¢	orange	25.00	25.00
BCL34	50¢	brown, die I	4.00	1.00
a		die II	10.00	6.00
b		pinperf	—	25.00
BCL35	$1	blue, die I	10.00	6.00
a		die II	4.00	0.50
b		die III	10.00	6.00
c		pinperf	50.00	30.00
d		double print	—	150.00
BCL36	$5	red brown	30.00	15.00
a		double print	—	150.00

1942-48 Eighth Series

Perf. 11¾ or 12½

Centre panel heavy borders on left and right sides.

	BCL38		BCL40	
BCL37	10¢	grey	2.00	1.50
a		perf. 12-1/2	4.00	2.50
b		hor. pr. imperf. between	200.00	—
c		cpl. offset on gum	125.00	—

			Uncan.	Used
BCL38	30¢	orange	5.00	5.00
a		hor. pr. imperf btwn	475.00	—
b		pinperf	—	35.00
BCL39	50¢	brown	3.50	1.00
a		perf. 12-1/2	6.00	2.00
b		hor. pr. imperf btwn	300.00	—
BCL40	$1	blue	4.00	0.75
a		hor. pr. imperf btwn	150.00	150.00
b		vert. pr. imperf btwn	150.00	—
c		pinperf	—	25.00

1948-57 Ninth Series
Horizontal and vertical shading in base of pedestal.
Sword casts a shadow.

		BCL41	BCL45	
BCL41	10¢	grey	3.50	2.50
a		double print	—	150.00
BCL42	50¢	olive brown	4.00	3.50
BCL43	$1	blue	6.00	1.00
BCL44	$2	red brown	10.00	3.50
BCL45	$2	magenta	10.00	3.50

1958 Centennial Issue
Centres are orange and green. Only color of borders is
given. Davac gum.

BCL46

BCL49

BCL46	10¢	grey	15.00	15.00
BCL47	25¢	red brown	25.00	25.00

			Uncan.	Used
BCL48	50¢	brown	12.50	12.50
a		orange omitted	875.00	875.00
BCL49	$1	blue	17.50	17.50
BCL50	$2	magenta	20.00	15.00

1958-70 Eleventh Series
Printed on Davac paper, dull gum. For used copies
compare paper with that used on Centennial Issue.

		BCL51	BCL57	
BCL51	10¢	grey	0.50	0.50
BCL52	50¢	olive brown	1.50	1.00
BCL53	$1	blue	2.00	1.00
BCL54	$2	magenta	4.00	2.25
BCL55	$3	orange	6.00	5.00
a		thick paper	25.00	10.00
BCL56	$5	red brown	10.00	6.00
BCL57	$10	light red	40.00	30.00
BCL58	$20	blue	50.00	45.00

1971-80 Twelfth Series
Rouletted

		BCL59	BCL62	
BCL59	$1	blue	3.50	3.50
a		horiz. pr. imperf between	350.00	—
BCL60	$2	magenta	6.00	5.00
a		horiz. pr. imperf between	450.00	—
b		imperf block of four	900.00	—
c		vert. pr. imperf between	450.00	—
BCL61	$5	red brown	15.00	10.00
BCL62	$30	turquoise	60.00	45.00

			Uncan.	Used

1981 Thirteenth Series
On Security paper with red & yellow underprint

	BCL65		BCL66	

BCL63	$1	blue (red)	10.00	5.00
a		imperf pair	200.00	—
BCL64	$5	brown	25.00	—
BCL65	$15	rose (red)	35.00	17.50
BCL66	$30	turquoise	60.00	50.00
a		davac gum	65.00	50.00
BCL67	$50	orange, davac	80.00	65.00

HOSPITAL AID TAX
1933
5% tax on meals

BCH1	3¢	black on orange	3.50	3.00
a		imperf between pair	250.00	—
b		2 rows swastikas at left	25.00	—
c		no swastikas at right	25.00	—
d		"3" open at bottom	10.00	—

CANADA REVENUE ALBUM

This 265 page album by E.S.J. van Dam was many years in the making and comes complete with 2 **Deluxe** high quality custom-designed three-ring binders. Each binder is gold imprinted with Volume Number and Queen Victoria, similar to FB52.

- Pages are printed on high quality water-marked paper

- Each page has Coat of Arms at the top.

- Matching blank pages and matching binders (without Volume Number) are available at additional cost.

Details from:
E.S.J. VAN DAM LTD.
OR YOUR
FAVOURITE DEALER

			Uncan.	Used
BCH2	4¢	black on pink	4.00	3.00
a		"4" no horiz. line at bottom	15.00	—

	BCH3		BCH5	

BCH3	5¢	black on brick	5.00	3.50
a		heavy offset on gum	25.00	—
b		"5" open at bottom	15.00	—
BCH4	10¢	black on red	25.00	4.50
a		"1" no horiz. bar at bottom	35.00	—
BCH5	$1	black on blue	75.00	45.00
a		"1" no horiz. bar at btm	100.00	—

POLICE INSPECTION STAMP
1927

BCP1

BCP1		black on orange	60.00	—
a		booklet pane of 12	750.00	—

DUCK STAMPS
1946
Designed by Ron Jackson

BCD1

BCD1	50¢	green & black, 1946	1500.	—
a		booklet pane of 4	6,000	—
b	50¢	black	2,000	—
c		BCD1 on license	—	—

	Uncan.	Used

1947
Same design as 1946.

BCD2

BCD2	50¢	yellow & blue, 1947	20.00	—
a		booklet pane of 4	85.00	—
b		book with 10 panes	850.00	—
c		on license	—	350.00

1948

BCD3

BCD3	$1	orange, green & blue	95.00	—
a		sheet of 5	500.00	—
b		imperf single	105.00	—
c		imperf sheet of 5	525.00	—
d		BCD3 on license	—	350.00

1949
Same design as 1948

BCD4

BCD4		orange, red & black	275.00	—
a		on hunting license	—	500.00
b		booklet pane of 5	1,350	—
c		booklet with 1 pane	1,500	—

	Uncan.	Used

1950-51
Decal type

BCD5

BCD5		multicolour decal	500.00	—
a		cpl. pane, tab at left	600.00	—

CANADA REVENUES

Our enormous revenue stock is available through our regular **"ReveNews"** bulletins or on approval against your want list.

We can supply most items listed in this catalogue, including many of the rarities. Many specialist items available on request.

REVENUE MAIL AUCTIONS HELD REGULARLY

• Lavishly illustrated auction catalogue only $2.00 or available by yearly subscription.

FOR FULL DETAILS
CONTACT

E.S.J. VAN DAM LTD.

BOX 300, BRIDGENORTH, ONTARIO
CANADA   K0L 1H0

Phone: (705) 292-7013
Fax: (705) 292-6311

BRITISH COLUMBIA TELEPHONE CO.

Issued in booklet panes of 4

1909

Type Set. Perf. 12. Issued with gum.

BCT1

			Uncan.	Used
BCT1	1909	black on light green	350.00	—

No Value - Dated

Issued with gum

			Uncan.	Used
BCT2	1909	black on green, A	400.00	—
BCT3	1910	green, series A	500.00	—
	a	watermarked	600.00	—

No Value - Various Undated Series

Issued without gum

BCT14

BCT29

			Uncan.	Used
BCT4	1909	brown, B	175.00	—
BCT5	1910	green, S.A.	125.00	—
BCT6	1911	green, S.B.	125.00	—
BCT7	1912	green, S.C.	125.00	—
BCT8	1913	green, S.D.	125.00	—
BCT9	1914	blue, S.E.	125.00	—
BCT10	1915	brown, S.F.	125.00	—
BCT11	1916	green, S.G.	125.00	—
BCT12	1917	blue, S.H.	95.00	—
BCT13	1918	green, S.I.	80.00	—
BCT14	1919	blue, S.J.	95.00	—
BCT15	1920	green, S.K.	120.00	—
BCT16	1921	brown, S.L.	120.00	—
BCT17	1922	green, S.M.	85.00	—
BCT18	1923	brown, S.N.	100.00	—
BCT19	1924	brown, S.P.	100.00	—
BCT20	1925	brown, S.Q.	100.00	—
BCT21	1926	green, S.R.	75.00	—

			Uncan.	Used
BCT22	1927	orange, S.S.	75.00	—
BCT23	1928	green, T.T.	70.00	—
BCT24	1929	violet, U.U.	75.00	—
BCT25	1930	green, V.V.	75.00	—
BCT26	1931	blue, W.W.	75.00	—
BCT27	1932	orange, X.X.	75.00	—
BCT28	1933	olive, Y.Y.	75.00	—
	a	watermarked	112.50	—
BCT29	1934	rose red, Z.Z.	75.00	—
	a	watermarked	112.50	—
BCT30	1935	purple, A.A.	75.00	—
	a	watermarked	112.50	—
BCT31	1936	brown red, B.B.	75.00	—
	a	hor. pair imprf betwn	375.00	—
BCT32	1937	steel blue, C.C.	75.00	—
BCT33	1938	green, D.D.	75.00	—
BCT34	1939	brown, E.E.	75.00	—
BCT35	1940	blue, F.F.	75.00	—
BCT36	1941	green, G.G.	75.00	—
BCT37	1942	orange, H.H.	75.00	—
	a	watermarked	112.50	—
BCT38	1943	purple, I.I.	75.00	—
BCT39	1944	red, J.J.	75.00	—
	a	watermarked	112.50	—
BCT40	1945	blue, K.K.	75.00	—
	a	watermarked	112.50	—
BCT41	1946	green, L.L.	80.00	—
BCT42	1947	slate lilac, M.M.	100.00	—

SMALL TELEPHONE FRANKS

1911-60

Panes of 6, except BCT43/45 are panes of 12.
Ungummed except for 1911 & 1913. Most can be found
watermarked - Add 50% to value.

BCT43

			Uncan.	Used
BCT43	5c	orange red, 1911	10.00	—
BCT44	25c	blue	15.00	—
	a	doubled control #	25.00	—
BCT45	$1	green	75.00	—
BCT46	5c	olive green, 1912	15.00	—
BCT47	25c	yellow brown	25.00	—
BCT48	$1	violet	75.00	—
BCT49	5c	black, 1913	50.00	—
BCT50	25c	red	50.00	—
BCT51	$1	brown	95.00	—
BCT52	5c	blue green, 1914	25.00	—
BCT53	25c	blue	35.00	—
BCT54	$1	olive green	50.00	—
BCT55	5c	red brown, 1915	15.00	—
BCT56	25c	vermilion	25.00	—
BCT57	$1	yellow brown	50.00	—
BCT58	5c	black, 1916	3.50	—
BCT59	25c	blue	20.00	—
BCT60	$1	green	45.00	—
BCT61	5c	brown, 1917	2.50	—
BCT62	25c	orange	5.00	—
BCT63	$1	olive green	25.00	—

			Uncan.	Used
BCT64	5c	blue, 1918	1.50	—
BCT65	25c	black	5.00	—
BCT66	$1	dark purple	25.00	—
BCT67	5c	green, 1919	1.50	—
BCT68	25c	red	2.50	—
BCT69	$1	dark brown	15.00	—
BCT70	5c	brown, 1920	3.50	—
BCT71	25c	blue	15.00	—
BCT72	$1	green	35.00	—
BCT73	5c	brown, 1921	1.50	—
BCT74	25c	venetian red	2.50	—
BCT75	$1	grey	20.00	—
BCT76	5c	green, 1922	15.00	—
BCT77	25c	yellow brown	25.00	—
BCT78	$1	blue	40.00	—
BCT79	5c	brown, 1923	15.00	—
BCT80	25c	purple	25.00	—
BCT81	$1	vermilion	65.00	—
BCT82	5c	green, 1924	1.50	—
BCT83	25c	blue	2.50	—
BCT84	$1	olive	25.00	—
BCT85	5c	yellow brown, 1925	50.00	—
BCT86	25c	red	50.00	—
BCT87	$1	brown	95.00	—
BCT88	5c	green, 1926	2.50	—
BCT89	25c	blue	3.50	—
BCT90	$1	purple	25.00	—
BCT91	5c	vermilion, 1927	3.00	—
BCT92	25c	light brown	6.00	—
BCT93	$1	dark brown	25.00	—
BCT94	5c	green, 1928	2.50	—
BCT95	25c	blue	10.00	—

BCT104   BCT108

			Uncan.	Used
BCT96	$1	violet	20.00	—
BCT97	5c	brown, 1929	3.50	—
BCT98	25c	vermilion	5.00	—
BCT99	$1	orange red	20.00	—
BCT100	5c	blue, 1930	2.00	—
BCT101	25c	olive	4.50	—
BCT102	$1	purple	17.50	—
BCT103	5c	orange, 1931	1.00	—
BCT104	25c	brown	2.00	—
BCT105	$1	green	6.00	—
BCT106	5c	green, 1932	1.50	—
BCT107	25c	violet	3.50	—
BCT108	$1	blue	15.00	—
BCT109	5c	rose, 1933	1.00	—
BCT110	25c	black	1.50	—
BCT111	$1	orange	10.00	—
BCT112	5c	violet, 1934	1.00	—
BCT113	25c	brown	1.75	—
BCT114	$1	green	7.50	—
BCT115	5c	brown, 1935	1.00	—
BCT116	25c	green	1.50	—
BCT117	$1	red	10.00	—
BCT118	5c	blue, 1936	1.00	—
a		double print	50.00	—
BCT119	25c	brown	1.50	—
BCT120	$1	black	7.50	—

			Uncan.	Used
BCT121	5c	red brown, 1937	1.25	—
BCT122	25c	green	1.50	—
BCT123	$1	red	10.00	—
BCT124	5c	orange, 1938	1.00	—
BCT125	25c	blue	1.50	—
BCT126	$1	red brown	25.00	—
BCT127	5c	blue, 1939	1.00	—
BCT128	25c	carmine	1.50	—
BCT129	$1	green	7.50	—
BCT130	5c	light green, 1940	1.00	—
BCT131	25c	black	1.50	—
BCT132	$1	red brown	7.50	—
a		vert. pr. impf. horiz.	175.00	—
BCT133	5c	violet, 1941	1.00	—
BCT134	25c	brown	1.50	—
BCT135	$1	blue	15.00	—
a		double print	50.00	—
b		joined "IT" variety	35.00	—
BCT136	5c	ultramarine, 1942	1.00	—
BCT137	25c	red	1.50	—
BCT138	$1	black	7.50	—
BCT139	5c	orange, 1943	1.00	—
BCT140	25c	green	1.50	—
BCT141	$1	brown	10.00	—
BCT142	5c	black, 1944	1.25	—
BCT143	25c	blue	1.75	—
BCT144	$1	purple	7.50	—
BCT145	5c	green, 1945	1.00	—
BCT146	25c	brown	1.50	—
BCT147	$1	red	7.50	—
BCT148	5c	violet, 1946	1.00	—
BCT149	25c	brown	1.75	—
BCT150	$1	blue	7.50	—
BCT151	5c	orange, 1947	1.00	—
BCT152	25c	green	1.75	—
BCT153	$1	black	7.50	—
BCT154	5c	brown, 1948	1.25	—
BCT155	25c	violet blue	1.75	—
BCT156	$1	red	7.50	—
BCT157	5c	orange, 1949	1.00	—
BCT158	25c	green	1.75	—
BCT159	$1	light blue	6.00	—
BCT160	5c	black, 1950	1.00	—
BCT161	25c	orange	1.75	—
BCT162	$1	dark green	6.00	—
BCT163	5c	blue, 1951	1.00	—
BCT164	25c	red brown	1.75	—
BCT165	$1	brown	7.50	—
BCT166	5c	brown, 1952	1.00	—
BCT167	25c	blue	1.75	—
BCT168	$1	red	7.50	—
BCT169	5c	purple, 1953	1.00	—
BCT170	25c	light green	5.00	—
BCT171	$1	olive yellow	25.00	—
BCT172	5c	brown, 1954	1.00	—
BCT173	25c	scarlet	1.75	—
BCT174	$1	blue	25.00	—
BCT175	5c	green, 1955	1.00	—
BCT176	25c	red orange	5.00	—
BCT177	$1	brown violet	25.00	—
BCT178	5c	black, 1956	1.00	—
BCT179	25c	turquoise	5.00	—
BCT180	$1	yellow	25.00	—
BCT181	5c	light blue, 1957	1.00	—
BCT182	25c	brown	3.75	—
BCT183	$1	green	20.00	—
BCT184	5c	orange, 1958	1.00	—
BCT185	25c	purple	1.75	—
BCT186	$1	carmine red	15.00	—
BCT187	5c	brown, 1959	1.00	—

			Uncan.	Used
BCT188	25c	green	1.75	—
BCT189	$1	black	25.00	—
BCT190	5c	yellow, 1960	2.50	—
BCT191	25c	red	5.00	—
BCT192	$1	blue	25.00	—

Year handstamped on basic 1960 stamps
1962 and 1963 blue overprint. Other years black overprint.

BCT193	5c	yellow, 1961	10.00	—
BCT194	25c	red	20.00	—
BCT195	$1	blue	45.00	—
BCT196	5c	yellow, 1962	10.00	—
BCT197	25c	red	20.00	—
BCT198	$1	blue	45.00	—
BCT199	5c	yellow, 1963	10.00	—

			Uncan.	Used
BCT200	25c	red	20.00	—
BCT201	$1	blue	45.00	—
BCT202	5c	yellow, 1964	10.00	—
BCT203	25c	red	20.00	—
BCT204	$1	blue	45.00	—
BCT205	5c	yellow, 1965	10.00	—
BCT206	25c	red	20.00	—
BCT207	$1	blue	45.00	—
BCT208	5c	yellow, 1966	10.00	—
BCT209	25c	red	20.00	—
BCT210	$1	blue	45.00	—
BCT211	5c	yellow, 1967	10.00	—
BCT212	25c	red	20.00	—
BCT213	$1	blue	45.00	—

PROVINCE OF MANITOBA

LAW STAMPS
1877 L S overprint
9 scallops

ML1   ML5

			Uncan.	Used
ML1	10c	green	7.50	4.00
ML2	20c	green	10.00	2.50
ML3	25c	green	50.00	25.00
ML4	50c	green	7.50	1.25
ML5	$1	green	30.00	5.00
ML6	$2	green	35.00	25.00

C F Overprint

ML7   ML11

			Uncan.	Used
ML7	10c	green	2.00	0.75
a		double overprint	75.00	75.00
ML8	20c	green	2.50	0.75
a		double overprint	95.00	95.00
ML9	25c	green	7.00	1.00
a		double overprint	—	75.00
ML10	50c	green	3.00	0.75
a		double overprint	—	75.00
ML11	$1	green	12.50	0.75
a		double overprint	—	125.00
ML12	$2	green	25.00	9.00

IMPERF PROVISIONALS
June 1877 On Thick Orange Paper
C F Overprint
Numbered & signed A. Begg

ML13

ML13	10c	red & black	—	250.00
ML14	20c	red & black	—	250.00
ML15	25c	red & black	—	250.00

Signed E.W. Romans

ML16	10c	red & black	—	500.00
ML17	20c	red & black	—	750.00
ML18	25c	red & black	—	500.00

		Uncan.	Used

October 1877
Initialled as shown

ML19

ML19	25c	red & black, E.W.R.	350.00	250.00
ML20	25c	red & black, D.C.	—	475.00
ML21	25c	red & black, DC & EWR	—	700.00
ML22	25c	as above, no initials	—	400.00

1881 WHITE PAPER
C F in Purple handstamp

ML26

ML23	10c	red & black	150.00	100.00
ML24	20c	red & black	200.00	125.00
ML25	50c	red & black	—	450.00
ML26	$1	red & black	350.00	300.00

C F in Indelible Pencil

ML27	10c	red & black	—	300.00
ML28	10c	initialled E.M.	—	600.00
a		LS in pen on CF	—	450.00

L S in Purple handstamp

ML29	10c	red & black	—	150.00
ML30	20c	red & black	—	450.00
ML31	50c	red & black	—	300.00
ML32	$1	red & black	—	150.00

L S in Indelible Pencil
Initialled E.M.

ML33	10c	red & black	—	500.00
ML34	50c	red & black	—	300.00
ML35	$1	red & black	—	500.00

1882
NINE SCALLOPS
Small C F on L S handstamped Top & Bottom

| ML36 | 10c | green | — | 300.00 |
| ML37 | 20c | green | — | 400.00 |

		Uncan.	Used

1884
L S stroked out - C F in ink

ML40a

ML38	10c	green	—	35.00
	a	LS not stroked out	—	30.00
ML39	20c	green	—	100.00
	a	LS not stroked out	—	100.00
ML40	25c	green	—	35.00
	a	LS not stroked out	—	30.00
ML41	50c	green	—	170.00
ML42	$1	green	—	110.00
ML43	$2	green	—	150.00

1884
C F stroked out - L S in ink

| ML44 | 50c | green | — | 100.00 |
| ML44A | 10c | C F in pen on ML1 | — | 325.00 |

1884
C F on L S - Vertical Handstamp
Large round C F

ML45

ML45	10c	green	30.00	17.50
ML46	20c	green	—	150.00
ML47	50c	green	30.00	17.50
	a	double "CF"	—	100.00

Small round C F - letters far apart

ML48	10c	green, red "CF"	—	85.00
	a	inverted red "CF"	—	125.00
ML49	50c	green, red "CF"	—	55.00
	a	purple "CF"	—	85.00

Tall thin C F - letters close together

| ML50 | 10c | green | 375.00 | 250.00 |

1885 SIX SCALLOPS
Perf. 12½
C F overprint

ML55

			Uncan.	Used
ML51	10c	blue green	250.00	75.00
ML52	20c	blue green	400.00	375.00
ML53	25c	blue green	250.00	350.00
ML54	50c	blue green	250.00	—
ML55	$1	blue green	700.00	40.00

Rouletted

ML56	10c	blue green	300.00	—

1866 NINE SCALLOPS
B F on L S

ML59   ML61

			Uncan.	Used
ML57	10c	green	—	95.00
ML58	20c	green	—	95.00
ML59	25c	green	12.50	4.50
a		"LS" doubled	—	150.00
ML60	50c	green	—	125.00
ML61	$1	green	60.00	30.00
a		BF on JF on LS	—	100.00
ML62	$2	green	—	165.00

ML64   ML68

B F on C F

			Uncan.	Used
ML63	10c	green	—	25.00
ML64	20c	green	35.00	25.00
ML65	25c	green	15.00	3.50
ML66	50c	green	20.00	15.00
ML67	$1	green	—	25.00
ML68	$2	green	25.00	20.00

1886 SIX SCALLOPS
B F on C F

ML71   ML72

			Uncan.	Used
ML69	10c	green	—	30.00
ML70	20c	green	—	40.00
ML71	25c	green	75.00	25.00
ML72	50c	green	35.00	7.50
ML73	$1	green	—	75.00

1887 NINE SCALLOPS
Handstamped B F

ML74   ML75

			Uncan.	Used
ML74	10c	green	55.00	20.00
a		violet/blue o/p	—	50.00
b		double overprint	—	—
c		error B on J of JF h/s	—	450.00
ML75	25c	green	75.00	35.00
a		violet/blue o/p	—	50.00
ML76	50c	green	—	30.00
a		additional JF o/p	—	—

1886
J F on L S

ML77	10c	green	35.00	25.00
ML78	20c	green	10.00	7.50
ML79	25c	green	10.00	3.50
a		double overprint	—	50.00
ML80	50c	green	—	25.00

Uncan.   Used

ML79   ML81
ML81 $1   green   7.50   2.50
ML82 $2   green   —   150.00

1886-92
J F on C F

ML83   ML88
ML83   10c   green   10.00   3.50
ML84   20c   green   6.00   1.75
ML85   25c   green   —   1.00
ML86   50c   green   —   2.00
ML87 $1   green   —   35.00
ML88 $2   green   200.00 120.00

1886-92 SIX SCALLOPS
J F on C F

ML89   ML93
ML89   10c   green   10.00   3.00
ML90   20c   green   40.00   35.00
ML91   25c   green   20.00   15.00
   a   double overprint   —   50.00
ML92   50c   green   7.50   4.00
ML93 $1   green   20.00   5.00

Uncan.   Used

1892 NINE SCALLOPS
J F in purple rubber stamp

ML94   ML94a
ML94   10c   green   6.00   0.75
   a   J F in violet/blue   60.00 50.00
   b   black overprint   —   50.00
ML95   20c   green   —   250.00
ML96   25c   green   5.50   0.75
ML97   50c   green   —   1.50
   a   J F in violet/blue   —   50.00
   b   double overprint   —   100.00
   c   black overprint   —   50.00
ML98 $1   green   —   100.00

J F Overprint - large blue letters

ML99   ML101
ML99   25c   green   10.00   5.00
ML100 50c   green   7.50   3.50
ML101 $1   green   15.00   2.50
   a   double overprint   —   100.00

J F Overprint - small blue letters

ML102   ML103
ML102 20c   green   6.00   3.00
ML103 50c   green   6.00   3.00

	Uncan.	Used

1892 NINE SCALLOPS

	ML104		ML108	
ML104	10c	green	5.00	2.00
ML105	20c	green	6.00	4.50
ML106	25c	green	4.00	1.00
ML107	50c	green	6.00	1.50
ML108	$1	green	65.00	15.00
ML109	$2	green	—	—

1897-1901 SIX SCALLOPS
Both colours come watermarked

	ML110		ML113	
ML110	10c	green	7.50	2.50
	a	blue green	10.00	2.50
	b	watermarked	65.00	20.00
	c	hor. pr. imperf between	—	400.00
ML111	25c	green	15.00	4.00
	a	blue green	15.00	3.50
	b	watermarked	75.00	35.00
ML112	50c	green	15.00	2.50
	a	blue green	7.50	2.50
	b	watermarked	50.00	30.00
	c	hor.pr. imperf between	—	400.00
ML113	$1	green	20.00	15.00
	a	blue green	30.00	25.00
	b	watermarked	150.00	60.00

SEARCH FEES

MS2

	Uncan.	Used

1921 "Provincial Secretary"
Similar to MS2, but "PAID" in thin letters, wide apart

MS1	25c	red	—	1,000

1928 "Provincial Secretary"

MS2	25c	red	—	800.00

1931 "Provincial Secretary"

MS3	50c	dark red	500.00	—
	a	50	on document	—	800.00

1950 "Provincial Secretary"

MS5

MS4	25c	red	60.00	55.00
MS5	50c	red	40.00	35.00
	a	on document	—	110.00

"Search"
Same type as MS3

MS6

MS6	50c	red	25.00	25.00

ca. 1960
On Davac paper

MS7	50c	red	—	25.00

ca. 1965
No vertical borders

MS8

MS8	50c	red	—	25.00

			Uncan.	Used

ca. 1967
Inscribed "Consumer & Corporate Affairs"

	MS9		MS10	
MS9	50c	red	25.00	20.00

1971.
Inscribed "Consumer, Corporate & Internal Services"

MS10	50c	red	10.00	10.00

Same design as previous issue, but "PAID" in smaller, thicker letters

MS11	50c	red	—	—
	a	horiz pair imperf between	225.00	—

A number of other Search Fees were issued by Manitoba and some Manitoba cities. Listings are under preparation

MANITOBA GOVERNMENT TELEPHONE FRANKS
Issued in Booklet Panes of 6.
Perf. 12, ungummed

	MT4		MT5	MT8	
MT1	5c	red, 1908		25.00	25.00
MT2	25c	blue		25.00	—
MT3	5c	red, 1909		20.00	—
	a	watermarked		35.00	—
MT4	25c	blue		20.00	20.00
MT5	5c	red, 1910		25.00	—
MT6	25c	blue		25.00	—

Issued in panes of 16.
Rouletted, ungummed

MT7	5c	brown lilac, 1911	10.00	—
	a	watermarked	15.00	—
	b	large "9" in 1911	30.00	—

			Uncan.	Used
MT8	25c	green	10.00	—
	a	watermarked	25.00	—
	b	large "9" in 1911	30.00	—

CITY OF WINNIPEG
Wildlife Conservation

	MW1			
MW1		turquoise	10.00	—
	a	vert. pr. imperf btwn	500.00	—

ELECTRICAL DEPARTMENT
Perf. 12

	MEL1			
MEL1	50c	blue	—	1000.

CITY OF ST. BONIFACE
Plumbing Department
Same design as MEL1

MP1	50c	light brown	—	500.00
MP2	$1	red	—	600.00
MP3	$2	brown	—	600.00

VACATION PAY STAMPS

	MV1		MV5	
MV1	1c	purple	7.50	—
	a	booklet pane of 10	75.00	—
MV2	2c	purple	7.50	15.00
	a	booklet pane of 10	85.00	—
MV3	5c	purple	25.00	25.00
	a	booklet pane of 10	275.00	—

| | Uncan. | Used | | | Uncan. | Used |

MV8

ME76

			Uncan.	Used
MV4	10c	purple	—	150.00
MV5	5c	blue	65.00	—
MV6	10c	brown	35.00	—
MV7	25c	orange	40.00	50.00
MV8	50c	rose red	100.00	—
MV9	$1	green	200.00	120.00
MV10	$5	yellow	325.00	—

MANITOBA OPERATING ENGINEERS & FIREMAN ACT
1958-76
Early issues are perforated.
Later issues rouletted.

Red – 1st Class
Blue – 2nd Class
Green – 3rd Class
Purple – Firemen & Refrigeration

The 1977 issue ME73-76 was printed but never issued.

ME2

		Uncan.	Used
ME1	red, 1958	—	—
ME2	blue	—	400.00
ME3	green	—	—
ME4	purple	—	—
ME5	red, 1959	—	—
ME6	blue	—	—
ME7	green	—	—
ME8	purple	—	—
ME9	red, 1960	—	—
ME10	blue	—	—
ME11	green	—	—
ME12	purple	—	—
ME13	red, 1961	—	—
ME14	blue	—	—
ME15	green	—	—
ME16	purple	—	—
ME17	red, 1962	—	—
ME18	blue	—	—
ME19	green	—	—
ME20	purple	—	—
ME21	red, 1963	—	—
ME22	blue	—	—
ME23	green	—	—

		Uncan.	Used
ME24	purple	—	—
ME25	red, 1964	—	—
ME26	blue	—	—
ME27	green	—	—
ME28	purple	—	—
ME29	red, 1965	—	—
ME30	blue	—	—
ME31	green	—	—
ME32	purple	—	—
ME33	red, 1966	—	—
ME34	blue	—	—
ME35	green	—	—
ME36	purple	—	—
ME37	red, 1967	—	—
ME38	blue	—	—
ME39	green	—	—
ME40	purple	—	—
ME41	red, 1968	—	—
ME42	blue	—	—
ME43	green	—	—
ME44	purple	—	—
ME45	rod, 1969	—	—
ME46	blue	—	—
ME47	green	—	—
ME48	purple	—	—
ME49	red, 1970	—	—
ME50	blue	—	—
ME51	green	—	—
ME52	purple	—	—
ME53	red, 1971	—	—
ME54	blue	—	—
ME55	green	—	—
ME56	purple	—	—
ME57	red, 1972	—	—
ME58	blue	—	—
ME59	green	—	—
ME60	purple	—	—
ME61	red, 1973	—	—
ME62	blue	—	—
ME63	green	—	—
ME64	purple	—	—
ME65	red, 1974	—	—
ME66	blue	—	—
ME67	green	—	—
ME68	purple	—	—
ME69	red, 1975	—	—
ME70	blue	—	—
ME71	green	—	—
ME72	purple	—	—
ME73	red, 1976	—	—
ME74	blue	—	—
ME75	green	—	—
ME76	purple	—	—

PROVINCE OF NEW BRUNSWICK

			Uncan.	Used
NBL9	20¢	vermilion	10.00	5.00
NBL10	50¢	brown red	35.00	25.00
NBL11	$1	violet	25.00	20.00
NBL12	$5	light green	40.00	15.00

LAW STAMPS
1884
Engraved, perf. 12

	NBL1		NBL4	
NBL1	10¢	blue	7.50	1.25
NBL2	20¢	blue	9.00	1.00
NBL3	50¢	blue	10.00	1.00
NBL4	$2	blue	15.00	1.25

1887-90
Engraved, perf. 12

	NBL5		NBL8	
NBL5	10¢	yellow	6.00	1.50
NBL6	20¢	vermilion	7.50	1.25
NBL7	50¢	brown	10.00	1.25
	a	chocolate	17.50	6.00
	b	strip of 3, impf vert.	—	1800.
NBL8	$5	deep green	85.00	65.00

1890-1900
Lithographed, perf. 12

NBL9 NBL11

1940
Lithographed, perf. 12

	NBL13		NBL17	
NBL13	10¢	yellow	2.50	2.50
NBL14	20¢	brown rust	2.50	2.50
NBL15	50¢	brown	3.50	3.50
NBL16	$1	purple	10.00	10.00
NBL17	$2	blue	12.00	10.00
NBL18	$5	green	25.00	20.00

Ca. 1977
Rouletted

NBL19

Existence of NBL19 and NBL24 has not been confirmed.

NBL19	10¢	yellow	—	—
NBL20	20¢	brown rust	2.50	—
NBL21	50¢	brown	2.50	—
NBL22	$1	purple	7.50	—
NBL23	$2	blue	15.00	—
NBL24	$5	green	—	—

	Uncan.	Used

PROBATE STAMPS
1895

NBP1   NBP5

Perf 11, 11¾, 12

			Uncan.	Used
NBP1	10¢	lemon yellow	20.00	15.00
NBP2	20¢	vermilion	20.00	12.50
NBP3	50¢	brown	15.00	12.50
NBP4	$2	blue	37.50	30.00
NBP5	$5	green	35.00	30.00
NBP6	$20	purple	65.00	60.00

Shading lines in hilt of dagger run upward from left to right. Upper and lower bars in "E" of PROBATE are the same length.

1915

Redrawn, lithographed
Perf 11¾, 12

Shading lines in hilt of dagger run downward from left to right. Upper bar of E of Probate shorter than lower bar.

NBP8

NBP7	10¢	yellow	55.00	40.00
NBP8	50¢	brown	40.00	25.00
NBP9	$2	blue	65.00	60.00
NBP10	$5	green	65.00	55.00
NBP11	$20	purple	110.00	65.00
a		imperf at right	—	75.00

NBP12   NBP13

1925

Engraved, perf. 11

			Uncan.	Used
NBP12	50¢	brown	85.00	75.00
NBP13	$5	green	125.00	100.00

1934

Lithographed, perf. 12

NBP14   NBP19

NBP14	10¢	brown	3.00	2.50
a		yellowish paper	3.00	—
NBP15	20¢	carmine	3.00	2.50
b		no graphics	3.00	—
NBP16	50¢	green	7.50	3.50
b		no graphics	7.50	—
NBP17	$2	orange	12.50	7.50
NBP18	$5	olive	25.00	15.00
b		no graphics	25.00	—
NBP19	$20	blue	65.00	40.00
NBP20	$100	black	375.00	150.00

Inscribed Canadian Bank Note Co. Ltd with graphic characters at beginning and end. The b #'s have no graphics.

Rouletted

NBP23

NBP21	10¢	brown	—	—
NBP22	20¢	carmine	2.50	—
NBP23	50¢	green	3.50	—
NBP24	$2	orange	—	—
NBP25	$5	olive	12.50	—
NBP26	$20	blue	40.00	—
NBP27	$100	black	200.00	—

The 10¢ & $2 have not been confirmed.

	Uncan.	Used

VACATION PAY STAMPS
1958
Engraved, perf. 12

NBV1   NBV3

			Uncan.	Used
NBV1	1¢	grey	5.00	—
NBV2	2¢	brown	5.00	—
NBV3	5¢	yellow	7.50	—
NBV4	10¢	green	10.00	—
NBV5	25¢	orange	15.00	—
NBV6	50¢	blue	20.00	—
NBV7	$1	red	25.00	—
NBV8	$5	purple	50.00	—

TOBACCO TAX
Watermarked = double catalogue
Issued in booklet panes of 4. without gum.

1940
Rouletted, value at left
Complete Panes sell @ 5x singles price.

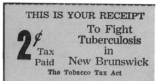

NBT2

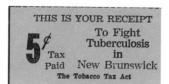

NBT4

NBT1	1¢	black on white	25.00	—
NBT2	2¢	black on yellow	30.00	—
NBT3	3¢	black on blue	7.50	—
NBT4	5¢	black on pink	5.00	—

Rouletted, value at right

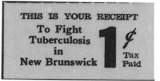

NBT5

	Uncan.	Used

NBT6

NBT5	1¢	black on white	100.00	—
NBT6	3¢	black on blue	150.00	—
a		perf 11¾	150.00	—

1940 Lorraine Cross
Rouletted

NBT7

NBT8

NBT7	1¢	red on white, shades	1.00	—
a		perf 11¾	35.00	—
b		imperf pane	20.00	—
NBT8	2¢	red on yellow	1.00	—
a		"TOBAOCO" error	5.00	—
b		imperf pane	20.00	—
NBT9	3¢	red on blue	1.00	—
a		imperf pane	20.00	—
NBT10	5¢	red on pink	—	—
a		imperf pane	20.00	—

1941 Coat of Arms
Rouletted

NBT11

NBT14

			Uncan.	Used
NBT11	1¢	red on white	1.00	—
a		perf 11 3/4	7.50	—
b		imperf pane	50.00	—
c		hor. pr. imperf betwn	35.00	—
NBT12	2¢	red on yellow	1.00	—
a		imperf pane	50.00	—
b		horiz. imperf pair	35.00	—
c		hor. pr. impf. vert.	35.00	—

			Uncan.	Used
NBT13	3¢	red on blue	1.00	—
a		horiz. imperf pair	35.00	—
b		hor. pr. imperf vert.	35.00	—
NBT14	5¢	red on pink	2.50	—
a		all red omitted	5.00	—
b		horiz. imperf pair	40.00	—
c		horiz pair imperf betwn	—	—

PROVINCE OF NEWFOUNDLAND

INLAND REVENUE
1898 QUEEN VICTORIA
Perf. 12

	NFR3		NFR9	
NFR1	5¢	red	85.00	75.00
NFR2	10¢	brown	75.00	50.00
NFR3	25¢	blue	15.00	10.00
NFR4	50¢	orange	35.00	25.00
NFR5	75¢	slate black	225.00	200.00
NFR6	$1	green	25.00	12.50
NFR7	$5	violet	75.00	50.00
NFR8	$20	brown	200.00	145.00
NFR9	$25	slate	375.00	295.00

1903 King Edward VII

	NFR10		NFR15	
NFR10	25¢	blue	15.00	7.50
a		watermarked	65.00	55.00
NFR11	50¢	black	200.00	125.00
a		watermarked	—	250.00

NFR12	$1	green	35.00	15.00
a		watermarked	—	200.00
b		very thick paper	—	50.00
NFR13	$5	lilac	—	75.00
NFR14	$50	violet brown	—	500.00
NFR15	$100	vermilion	400.00	225.00
a		perf 11¾	400.00	255.00

1910 King George V
Perf. 11, 12

	NFR16		NFR20	
NFR16	5¢	vermilion	5.00	2.50
a		perf 11	3.00	1.25
b		watermarked	—	100.00
NFR17	10¢	olive green	6.00	2.50
a		perf 11	4.50	1.25
b		watermarked	—	100.00
NFR18	25¢	blue	6.00	3.50
a		perf 11	3.50	1.25
b		watermarked	—	150.00
NFR19	50¢	black	15.00	4.50
a		perf 11	20.00	7.50
b		watermarked	—	100.00
NFR20	$1	green	15.00	3.50
a		perf 11	22.50	6.00
b		watermarked	—	100.00
NFR21	$5	violet (shades)	35.00	30.00
a		perf 11	—	65.00
b		perf 11 x 12	150.00	125.00
c		perf 12 x 11	—	150.00
NFR22	$20	yellow brown	100.00	50.00
NFR23	$25	salmon	—	150.00
a		perf 11	225.00	175.00

	Uncan.	Used

Similar to 1910 Issue.
No bank note co. imprint.

	NFR24			NFR25	
NFR24	50¢	black	35.00	15.00
NFR25	$1	green	35.00	17.50

1938 Caribou
Perf. 13¾, 14¼

	NFR26			NFR30	
NFR26	5¢	vermilion	3.50	2.25
NFR27	10¢	black	3.50	2.50
NFR28	25¢	green	4.00	3.00
NFR29	50¢	blue	25.00	15.00
NFR30	$1	brown	15.00	7.50
NFR31	$2.50	mustard	35.00	25.00
NFR32	$5	green	75.00	60.00
NFR33	$20	brown	—	250.00
NFR34	$50	orange	—	250.00
NFR35	$100	claret	—	550.00

1943 Caribou
Perf. 12

	NFR37			NFR42	
NFR36	5¢	red	2.00	1.00
	a	gutter pair	75.00	—
NFR37	10¢	black	2.50	1.00
	a	gutter pair	200.00	—
NFR38	25¢	green	3.00	1.00
	a	gutter pair	300.00	—
NFR39	50¢	blue	5.00	1.50
NFR40	$1	brown	2.50	1.00
NFR41	$2.50	mustard	25.00	25.00
NFR42	$5	green	15.00	5.00
NFR43	$20	brown	60.00	20.00

	Uncan.	Used

1963. PROVISIONALS

	NFR44			NFR45	
NFR44	5	on 25¢ green	95.00	95.00
	a	gutter pair	250.00	—
NFR45		manuscript "5"	—	25.00
	a	on document	—	95.00
	b	NFR45 + blue 5¢, signed	—	500.00

ca. 1969 CARIBOU
Perf. 13, 13¼, 13½

	NFR46			NFR48	
NFR46	5¢	red	0.50	0.50
	a	gutter pair	7.50	—
NFR47	10¢	black	0.50	0.50
	a	gutter pair	7.50	—
NFR48	25¢	green	1.00	1.00
	a	gutter pair	10.00	—
NFR49	50¢	blue	2.50	1.50
NFR50	$1	brown	5.00	2.00
NFR51	$2.50	mustard	10.00	5.00
NFR52	$5	green	15.00	7.50
NFR53	$20	brown	45.00	10.00

MONEY ORDER TAX
1914
Perf. 14 x 12

	NFM1			NFM1a	
NFM1	5¢	ultramarine	12.50	12.50
	a	no "." after "only"	12.50	12.50
	b	broken "Y" in MONEY	15.00	15.00
	c	NFM1a+1b combined	30.00	30.00
Overprinted sideways "MONEY ORDER" in caps				
NFM2			—	750.00

	Uncan.	Used			Uncan.	Used

CUSTOMS DUTY
1925 Edward VIII
Rouletted 7

	NFC1				
		NFC1		NFC2	
NFC1	1¢	green		1.50	1.25
NFC2	3¢	orange brown		2.50	1.50
NFC3	5¢	violet		3.00	2.00

1938. Caribou
Perf. 12

	NFC4		NFC5		
NFC4	1¢	green		2.25	2.00
NFC5	5¢	red violet		3.50	3.00

TRANSPORTATION TAX
1927

NFT2

NFT1	$1	green	5500.	—
NFT2	$2	red	2750.	2500.
NFT3	$3	blue	3500.	3000.

BEER STAMP
1938

Perf. 12 x 13¼
Issued without gum

NFB1

NFB1	10/12¢	blue	1500.	1500.
	a	p. 14 x 14 x 14 x 13	2500.	—

WAR SAVINGS 1940
Used copies must have proper cancel.

NFW1

NFW1	10¢	blue	20.00	—

NATIONAL SAVINGS 1947

	NFW2		NFW3		
NFW2	10¢	red		75.00	—
NFW3	10¢	blue		15.00	—

"NEWFOUNDLAND SAVINGS BANK"
Overprint in red

NFW4

NFW4	10¢	blue, light red o/p	5.00	50.00
	a	dark red o/p	5.00	—
	b	yellowish paper	5.00	—

PROVINCE OF NOVA SCOTIA

Uncan. Used

BILL STAMPS
1868. Federal Bill Stamps
Overprinted "N.S." for use in Nova Scotia.
Perf 12, 11½ x 12, rough perf. 12½

		NSB1	NSB11	NSB18a	
NSB1	1¢	brown		5.00	2.50
NSB2	1¢	orange		1,000	750.00
NSB3	2¢	orange		5.00	2.50
NSB4	3¢	green		5.00	2.50
NSB5	4¢	brown		15.00	6.00
a		imprf margin at right		—	—
NSB6	5¢	orange		15.00	6.00
NSB7	6¢	green		12.50	4.00
a		double overprint		—	500.00
b		pair 1 with double o/p		—	650.00
NSB8	7¢	orange		20.00	15.00
NSB9	8¢	brown		25.00	15.00
NSB10	9¢	green		10.00	2.50
NSB11	10¢	blue		15.00	2.50
NSB12	20¢	blue		15.00	4.50
a		rough perf 12½		250.00	225.00
b		double overprint		—	400.00
NSB13	30¢	blue		15.00	5.00
NSB14	40¢	blue		20.00	12.50
NSB15	50¢	blue		50.00	25.00
NSB16	$1	blue & black		175.00	150.00
a		rough perf 12 1/2		150.00	125.00
NSB17	$2	red & black		225.00	200.00
a		double overprint		—	400.00
NSB18	$3	green & black		350.00	300.00
a		rough perf 12 1/2		110.00	110.00

HALIFAX LAW LIBRARY
1879
Perf. 12½. Size 19 x 23½ mm.

NSH1

NSH1	25¢	dark green	12.50	4.50

Ca. 1890
Perf. 14. Size 19½ x 24½ mm.

NSH2	25¢	dark green	12.50	4.50
a		watermarked	—	35.00

Uncan. Used

NSH2 NSH2b

			Uncan.	Used
b		imperf	—	125.00
c		major plate scratch	—	35.00
d		NSH2c on NSH2a	—	75.00
NSH3	50¢	dark green	12.50	4.00
a		watermarked	—	35.00

1910 Re-engraved
Size 20 x 25 mm. Perf. 14
Vertical lines to left of "HALIFAX" unbroken white dots around scrolls are larger & have green centres, etc.

NSH4

NSH4	50¢	green	25.00	7.50
a		watermarked	—	50.00
b		double print	—	150.00

ca. 1940's
Perf. 12. "HALIFAX" 6½ mm long and 1 mm tall

NSH5	(50¢)	green	20.00	12.00

NSH5

ca. 1955
New die. "HALIFAX" 5 mm long and ½ mm tall.
Thin vertical lines much closer together. No shading in forearm to left of scale, etc.

Uncan. Used

NSH6

NSH6	(50¢)	green	20.00	6.00
	a	double print	—	150.00

ca. 1956
"$1" Overprint on NSH5

NSH7	$1	scarlet	70.00	30.00

NSH7   NSH7a

	a	$1	rose carmine	70.00	30.00
	b		double overprint	100.00	80.00

Late 1960's
Red $3.00 overprint, "0" in $3.00 is rectangular

NSH8	$3	on NSH6	55.00	45.00

NSH8

1970's
Red $3.00 overprint. Larger, Rounder numerals

NSH9	$3	on NSH6	65.00	60.00

1979
Red $3 Overprint, Rouletted, Davac gum

NSH10   NSH11

NSH10	$3	on olive green	15.00	—

1987
Red $3 overprint, perf 11¾
Sheets of 25, Davac gum, perfs. on all sides

NSH11	$3	on green	7.50	—

1989
Sheets of 25, perf. 12 x 11¾

NSH12	$3	on olive	7.50	—

Margin stamps have 1 or 2 straight edges.

CAPE BRETON

LAW STAMPS
1903 PROVISIONALS

	Uncan.	Used

NSC2

Tall stamp with handstamped crown, circle and value. Thick red border

NSC1	25¢	blue	—	725.00
NSC2	50¢	purple	—	950.00

Square on white paper

NSC3	25¢	"LAW STAMP"	—	500.00

1904 PROVISIONALS
Octagonal border

NSC4

NSC4	25¢	"LAW STAMP"	—	400.00
NSC5	25¢	"BAR LIBRARY"	—	400.00
NSC6	25¢	"LAW LIBRARY"	—	450.00
NSC7	50¢	"LAW STAMP"	—	550.00
NSC8	50¢	"LAW LIBRARY"	—	400.00

Rounded corner border

NSC9

Uncan.   Used   Uncan.   Used

Handstamped NEW VALUES on 1955 issue

NSC11

NSC9	25¢	"LAW STAMP"	—	375.00
NSC10	25¢	typed denomination	—	375.00
NSC11	50¢	"LAW STAMP"	—	375.00

NSC20   NSC21

NSC22   NSC23

1904
Coloured background
Perf. 11¾

NSC20	$1.00	on NSC16	50.00	—
NSC21	$1.00	on NSC17	50.00	—
NSC22	$3.00	on NSC16	50.00	—
NSC23	$3.00	on NSC17	50.00	—

Issued in sheets of 12, Rouletted, Davac gum.

| NSC24 | $1 | black on yellow | 3.00 | — |
| NSC25 | $3 | black on turq. green | 7.50 | — |

NSC12   NSC13

| NSC12 | 25¢ | red | 175.00 | 125.00 |
| NSC13 | 50¢ | blue | 200.00 | 150.00 |

VACATION PAY STAMPS
1958
Perf. 11

1923
White Background
Perf. 11¾ x 12½

NSV1   NSV6

NSV1	1¢	yellow	10.00	7.50
NSV2	5¢	carmine	10.00	7.50
NSV3	10¢	violet	15.00	10.00
NSV4	25¢	blue	20.00	15.00
NSV5	50¢	brown	35.00	25.00
NSV6	$1	green	60.00	50.00
NSV7	$5	orange	125.00	85.00

NSC14   NSC15

| NSC14 | 25¢ | red | 150.00 | 110.00 |
| NSC15 | 50¢ | blue | 175.00 | 125.00 |

1955
Perf. 11¾, lithographed

GAME STAMP
Perf. 12½

NSC17   NSC18

NSC16	25¢	red	10.00	—
NSC17	50¢	green	10.00	—
NSC18	$1	carmine	20.00	—
NSC19	$3	blue	175.00	—

NSG1

| NSG1 | | green, pheasant | 100.00 | — |

PROVINCE OF ONTARIO

			Uncan.	Used

LAW STAMPS
1864 Law Stamps
Perf. 12
Perce en scie, rouletted and combinations thereof.
Overprinted "C.F." in blue.
"C.F. = CONSOLIDATED FUND"

	OL2		OL13a	
OL1	5¢	green	6.00	1.50
OL2	10¢	green	3.00	0.35
a		"C.F." omitted	—	185.00
b		black blue o/p	—	25.00
OL3	20¢	green	7.50	2.00
OL4	30¢	green	12.50	5.00
OL5	40¢	green	10.00	5.00
OL6	50¢	green	7.50	0.75
OL7	60¢	green	15.00	10.00
OL8	70¢	green	20.00	12.50
OL9	80¢	green	20.00	10.00
OL10	90¢	green	35.00	25.00
a		rouletted	250.00	—
OL11	$1	green & black	25.00	2.50
OL12	$2	green & black	35.00	10.00
OL13	$3	green & black	65.00	60.00
a		rouletted	250.00	—
OL14	$4	green & black	70.00	70.00
OL15	$5	green & black	70.00	70.00
a		rouletted	250.00	—

Overprinted "F.F" in yellow
F.F. = Fee Fund

OL16   OL28

			Uncan.	Used
OL16	5¢	rouletted	40.00	—
OL17	10¢	green	3.00	0.35
OL18	20¢	green	3.50	0.40
a		bisect on document	—	750.00
OL19	30¢	green	4.00	0.45
OL20	40¢	green	5.00	0.75
a		double overprint	—	200.00
OL21	50¢	green	3.50	0.75
OL22	60¢	green	7.50	0.75
OL23	70¢	green	75.00	75.00
a		rouletted	350.00	—
OL24	80¢	green	20.00	17.50
OL25	90¢	green	45.00	40.00
a		rouletted	350.00	—
OL26	$1	green & black	25.00	6.00
OL27	$2	green & black	30.00	22.50
a		rouletted	350.00	—
OL28	$3	green & black	55.00	50.00
a		rouletted	350.00	—
OL29	$4	green & black	70.00	70.00
OL30	$5	green & black	70.00	70.00

Overprinted "L.S." in carmine
L.S.= Law Society

OL31	5¢	rouletted	40.00	—
a		imperf	50.00	—

OL32   OL41

OL32	10¢	rouletted	40.00	—
OL33	20¢	green	3.50	0.75
a		brown "L.S."	—	25.00
OL34	30¢	green	11.00	5.00
OL35	40¢	green	15.00	5.00
a		rouletted	350.00	—
OL36	50¢	green	6.00	1.00
a		brown "L.S."	—	25.00
OL37	60¢	green	7.00	1.25
OL38	70¢	green	60.00	55.00
a		rouletted	350.00	—
OL39	80¢	green	50.00	45.00
OL40	90¢	green	50.00	50.00
a		rouletted	350.00	—
OL41	$1	green & black	25.00	4.00
a		maroon "L.S."	50.00	30.00
b		bisect on document	—	750.00
OL42	$2	green & black	30.00	5.00
a		brown "L.S."	50.00	30.00
b		missing "." after L.S	—	150.00
OL43	$3	green & black	50.00	45.00
a		rouletted	350.00	—
OL44	$4	green & black	50.00	45.00

			Uncan.	Used
OL45	$5	green & black	50.00	45.00
a		rouletted	350.00	—

1869-1911 Law Stamps

**Perf. 11,12,11½,12½ & combinations thereof.
Many shades**

	OL46		OL57	
OL46	5¢	red	5.00	3.00
OL47	10¢	red	0.75	0.25
a		vert.pr.imperf betwn	—	500.00
OL48	20¢	red	0.75	0.25
a		vert.pr.imperf betwn	—	450.00
b		stitch watermark	—	150.00
c		single imperf vertically	—	125.00
OL49	30¢	red	0.75	0.25
OL50	30¢	green	125.00	95.00
a		stitch watermark	—	150.00
OL51	40¢	red	1.00	0.25
OL52	50¢	red	1.25	0.25
a		vert.pr.imperf betwn	—	300.00
OL53	60¢	red	2.50	0.75
OL54	70¢	red	6.00	6.00
OL55	80¢	red	6.00	6.00
OL56	90¢	red	10.00	10.00
OL57	$1	red	2.00	0.25
OL58	$2	red	3.75	0.50
OL59	$3	red	7.50	6.00
OL60	$4	red	60.00	12.50

1904 Law Stamps

Perf. 11, 12

	OL61		OL64	
OL61	$4	green on green paper	4.50	4.50
OL62	$5	blue	10.00	10.00
OL63	$10	orange	10.00	10.00
OL64	$20	brown	20.00	20.00
OL65	$50	purple	50.00	50.00

		Uncan.	Used

1929-40 Law Stamps

Perf. 11

	OL66		OL74	
OL66	5¢	violet	5.00	4.00
OL67	10¢	green	0.50	0.25
OL68	20¢	black	1.00	0.25
OL69	20¢	yellow	0.75	0.25
OL70	30¢	black	1.00	0.25
OL71	30¢	indigo	1.75	0.60
OL72	50¢	olive green	1.75	0.50
OL73	50¢	red	2.00	0.50
OL74	$1	orange red	3.50	0.45
OL75	$1	blue on flesh	2.50	0.50
OL76	$2	brown	6.00	0.75
OL77	$2	blue/pale turquoise	5.00	0.50
OL78	$3	yellow brown	8.50	1.50
OL79	$3	blue on green	7.00	1.00
OL80	$3	blue on blue	8.50	3.50
OL81	$4	grey	15.00	7.50
OL82	$4	blue on orange	9.50	0.50
OL83	$5	red brown	15.00	12.50
OL84	$5	blue on blue	12.50	2.50
OL85	$5	sepia	15.00	12.50
OL86	$10	red	35.00	25.00
OL87	$10	blue	25.00	25.00
OL88	$10	blue on red	25.00	12.50
OL89	$50	dark brown	175.00	175.00
OL90	$50	blue on orange	350.00	175.00

STOCK TRANSFER TAX STAMPS

1910-26

Perf. 12

	OST1a		OST12	
OST1	2¢	pale red	0.75	0.60
a		carmine	0.75	0.60
OST2	3¢	on 2c overprint	1.50	1.00
OST3	3¢	green	1.00	0.65
OST4	10¢	dark green	7.50	5.00
OST5	15¢	bistre brown	0.75	0.45
OST6	20¢	bistre brown	15.00	8.50
a		dark brown	7.50	5.00
OST7	30¢	blue	1.00	0.45
OST8	50¢	purple	17.50	15.00
a		dull mauve	17.50	15.00

			Uncan.	Used
OST9	60¢	olive green	2.50	0.75
OST10	$1	blue	17.50	15.00
OST11	$1.50	red	5.00	2.50
OST12	$2	olive green	40.00	30.00
OST13	$3	brown	10.00	3.50
OST14	$10	orange	60.00	40.00
OST15	$15	violet	35.00	10.00

1926
Luxury Tax Stamps Overprinted "STOCK TRANSFER" Tax in black.

	OST16		OST17	
OST16	3¢	on 2 1/2 mills	1.50	1.00
	a	"TRANSFE" error	50.00	50.00
	b	"TRANSF" error	—	50.00
OST17	6¢	blue	2.50	1.50

1935 Horizontal format.
Perf. 11

	OST18		OST26	
OST18	1¢	orange	1.50	0.50
OST19	2¢	carmine	1.75	0.75
OST20	4¢	olive green	1.75	1.50
OST21	5¢	blue on pink	2.50	0.75
OST22	10¢	black	1.75	1.00
OST23	15¢	brown	3.00	1.50
OST24	30¢	bistre	3.50	1.50
OST25	50¢	green	4.00	1.00
OST26	$1	red on white	35.00	30.00
OST27	$1.50	blue on orange	35.00	35.00
OST28	$2	dark blue on blue	40.00	35.00
OST29	$3	blue on pink	45.00	40.00
OST30	$3	black on blue	200.00	175.00
OST31	$60	dark green on yellow	150.00	65.00

1936-40 Vertical format
Perf. 11

OST32	OST33

			Uncan.	Used
OST32	25¢	red brown	6.50	3.50
OST33	$1	blue on flesh	15.00	10.00
OST34	$2	blue on blue	30.00	15.00
OST35	$5	blue on green	45.00	30.00
OST36	$10	blue on red	40.00	20.00

Overprints

	OST37		OST39	
OST37	1¢	on 25c (OST32)	30.00	—
OST38	10¢	on 25c (OST32)	55.00	—
	a	double overprint	250.00	—
OST39	$1	on 2c (OST19)	475.00	—
OST40	$10	on $15 (OST15)	950.00	—

LUXURY TAX STAMPS
1926
lithographed, rouletted

	OLT1		OLT3		OLT6	
OLT1	2½ mills	on 2m red brown	15.00	15.00		
OLT2	2½ mills	red brown	0.75	0.75		
OLT3	1¢	on 1m green	5.00	5.00		
OLT4	1¢	green	2.00	2.00		
OLT5	6¢	blue	3.50	3.50		
OLT6	50¢	orange	15.00	—		

Law Stamp
OVERPRINTED in black "LUXURY TAX"

			OLT7	
OLT7	50¢	orange (OL52)	15.00	—

			Uncan.	Used

GASOLINE TAX
1928 Ontario Law stamps
Overprinted "GASOLINE TAX"
Perf. 11, 12, 12 x 11½

	OGT2			
	OGT9			
OGT1	3¢	on 5c red	10.00	—
OGT2	3¢	on 40c red	10.00	—
OGT3	3¢	on 50c red	10.00	—
OGT4	3¢	on 60c red	10.00	—
OGT5	3¢	on 70c red	10.00	—
OGT6	15¢	on 60c red	15.00	—
OGT7	15¢	on 70c red	15.00	—
OGT8	15¢	on 80c red	15.00	—
OGT9	15¢	on 90c red	20.00	50.00

Luxury Tax stamps
Overprinted "GASOLINE TAX" + New Value

	OGT11			
	OGT16			
OGT10	5¢	red on 1c green	200.00	—
OGT11	5¢	purple on 1c green	50.00	—
OGT12	6¢	red on 1c green	50.00	50.00
OGT13	6¢	purple on 1c green	50.00	50.00
OGT14	25¢	red on 6c blue	50.00	—
OGT15	25¢	purple on 6c blue	50.00	50.00
OGT16	30¢	red on 6c blue	90.00	—
OGT17	30¢	purple on 6c blue	—	110.00
OGT18	6¢	blue, red bar o/p	150.00	—
OGT19	OST11	o/p red GASOLINE TAX	650.00	—
OGT20	OST13	purple GASOLINE TAX	750.00	—

VACATION PAY STAMPS
ca. 1955

OV1	OV10

			Uncan.	Used
OV1	1¢	brown & black	1.00	1.00
a		wide gutter pair	25.00	—
OV2	2¢	brown & black	1.00	1.00
OV3	3¢	brown & black	3.00	3.00
a		wide gutter pair	25.00	—
OV4	4¢	brown & black	3.00	3.00
a		wide gutter pair	25.00	—
OV5	5¢	brown & black	3.00	3.00
a		wide gutter pair	25.00	—
OV6	10¢	brown & black	3.50	3.00
a		wide gutter pair	25.00	—
OV7	25¢	brown & black	6.00	5.00
OV8	50¢	brown & black	15.00	12.50
a		pair, value omitted on 1	400.00	—
OV9	$1	brown & black	200.00	200.00
OV10	$1	red & black	30.00	20.00
a		pair, value omitted on 1	400.00	—
b		deformed $ sign	45.00	40.00
OV11	$5	blue & black	60.00	30.00

PROVINCE OF PRINCE EDWARD ISLAND

TOBACCO TAX
Issued in booklet panes of 4. no gum, except PET1b which has gum.

1942 Tobacco tax
Rouletted

PET2

PET1	1¢	green on yellow	2.50	—
a		green on buff	7.50	—
b		green on orange	15.00	—
PET1 c		arrow in "your"	7.50	—
PET2	2¢	red, smooth print	1.50	—
a		red, coarse print	1.50	—
b		red on buff	10.00	—
c		lake on white	35.00	—
d		"yojr" error	10.00	—
PET3	3¢	black on pink	55.00	—
PET4	3¢	blue on light green	1.75	—
a		blue on grey green	1.75	—
b		blue on blue green	1.75	—
c		missing Y in "YOUR"	10.00	—
PET5	3¢	double print	7.50	—
PET6	4¢	black on pink	15.00	—

Watermarked copies = 2x single stamp price.
Complete panes priced at 5x single stamp price.

1765 AMERICA EMBOSSED REVENUES

March 22,1765 to May 1, 1766. Used at Montreal & Quebec city. Many other values exist, but they were apparently only used in the south (USA). These are the same as the British embossed with simply the word "AMERICA" added at the top. Impressions are colourless and were impressed directly on the document.

QAE1

			Cut Square	Document
QAE1	3p	die A	750.00	1250.
QAE2	3p	die B	1750.	2000.

			Cut Square	Document
QAE3	4p	die A	—	—
QAE4	6p	die A	—	2250.
QAE5	6p	die B	1750.	2000.
QAE6	1/-	die A	750.00	1200.
QAE7	1/6	die A	750.00	1000.
QAE8	2/-	die B	—	2500.
	a	die A	—	—
QAE9	2/3	die A	1000.	1250.
QAE10	2/3	die B	1000.	—
QAE11	2/6	die A	600.00	750.00
QAE12	4/-		—	2000.
QAE13	5/-		—	—
QAE14	10/-		—	2500.

Items not priced have not appeared on the market and no pricing information is available. This issue was actually for all of Canada, but since copies have been recorded only in Quebec, they have been listed in the Quebec section of this catalogue.

PROVINCE OF QUEBEC

LAW STAMPS
1864 Lower Canada
Overprinted "L.C." in red.

QL1   QL10

Perf. 12, thin & thick paper.

QL16   QL25

			Uncan.	Used
QL1	10¢	green	7.50	1.00
QL2	20¢	green	7.50	1.50
QL3	30¢	green	7.50	2.50
QL4	40¢	green	10.00	3.50
QL5	50¢	green	10.00	1.00
QL6	60¢	green	20.00	7.50
QL7	70¢	green	25.00	9.00
QL8	80¢	green	20.00	2.50
QL9	90¢	green	40.00	15.00
QL10	$1	green & black	20.00	1.50
QL11	$2	green & black	30.00	3.50
QL12	$3	green & black	40.00	15.00
QL13	$4	green & black	50.00	10.00
QL14	$5	green & black	65.00	7.50

1871-90 Law Stamps
Perf. 11½, 12 and combination
Many different shades

			Uncan.	Used
QL15	10¢	red	2.50	0.25
QL16	20¢	red	3.00	0.25
QL17	30¢	red	5.00	0.25
QL18	40¢	red	4.00	0.25
QL19	50¢	red	4.50	0.25
QL20	60¢	red	5.00	0.50
QL21	70¢	red	7.00	0.75
QL22	80¢	red	7.00	0.75
QL23	90¢	red	8.00	2.75
QL24	$1	blue	7.50	0.45
QL25	$2	blue	20.00	0.65
QL26	$3	blue	20.00	3.50
QL27	$4	blue	30.00	3.00
QL28	$5	blue	40.00	2.00
QL29	$10	yellow	—	75.00
QL30	$20	green	—	85.00
QL31	$30	slate purple	—	100.00

1893-1906 Law Stamps
Perf. 12, shades range from grey to violet

			Uncan.	Used
QL32	10¢	grey violet	1.50	0.25
QL33	20¢	grey violet	1.75	0.25
QL34	30¢	grey violet	1.50	0.35
QL35	40¢	grey violet	1.50	0.25
QL36	50¢	grey violet	1.50	0.25
	a	light brown	—	15.00
QL37	60¢	grey violet	—	0.75
QL38	70¢	grey violet	—	0.75
QL39	70¢	blue	—	6.00
QL40	80¢	grey violet	—	0.75

		Uncan.	Used

	QL32		QL43	
QL41	80¢	blue	6.50	3.00
QL42	90¢	grey violet	—	0.75
QL43	$1	green	6.50	0.25
QL44	$1	carmine	—	35.00
QL45	$2	green	10.00	1.25
QL46	$2	brown	—	10.00
QL47	$3	green	10.00	1.75
QL48	$3	orange	—	45.00
QL49	$4	green	—	6.00
QL50	$4	brown	—	40.00
QL51	$5	green	12.50	0.75
QL52	$5	carmine	—	35.00
QL53	$10	blue	17.50	6.00
QL54	$20	yellow	—	8.50
QL55	$30	vermilion	—	12.50

1912 Law Stamps
Perf. 11, 12, great variety of shades

	QL56		QL70	
QL56	10¢	green	5.00	0.25
a		hairlines	15.00	5.00
QL57	20¢	blue	5.00	0.25
a		hairlines	6.00	1.25
QL58	30¢	orange	5.00	0.25
QL59	40¢	brown	5.00	0.50
QL60	50¢	black	7.50	0.25
a		hairlines	6.00	2.00
QL61	60¢	olive	7.50	0.75
QL62	70¢	bistre	7.50	1.75
QL63	80¢	brown	10.00	2.00
a		hairlines	—	5.00
QL64	90¢	red brown	15.00	5.00
QL65	$1	red	15.00	0.25
a		orange	25.00	0.25
QL66	$2	purple	25.00	3.50
a		hairlines	—	10.00
QL67	$3	green	25.00	7.50
QL68	$4	grey	30.00	7.50
QL69	$5	blue	35.00	6.00

			Uncan.	Used
QL70	$10	violet brown	75.00	70.00
QL71	$20	red brown	150.00	150.00
QL72	$30	olive	100.00	80.00

1924 "HONORAIRES-FEES"
Overprint on 1912 Law Stamps
Overprints come 17½ and 18½ mm long.

	QL75		QL83	
QL73	10¢	green	5.00	0.25
a		hairlines	15.00	5.00
QL74	20¢	blue	5.00	0.25
a		hairlines	6.00	1.25
b		bluish paper	5.00	0.35
QL75	30¢	orange	5.00	0.25
a		inverted overprint	—	650.00
QL76	40¢	brown	5.00	0.65
QL77	50¢	black	5.00	0.25
a		hairlines	6.00	1.25
b		inverted overprint	—	650.00
QL78	60¢	olive	15.00	5.00
QL79	70¢	bistre	10.00	4.50
a		inverted overprint	—	650.00
QL80	80¢	brown	10.00	3.75
a		hairlines	15.00	5.00
b		strong re-entry	—	150.00
QL81	90¢	red brown	15.00	5.00
QL82	$1	red (shades)	4.50	0.65
a		inverted overprint	—	650.00
b		brown overprint	—	50.00
c		orange	7.50	0.75
QL83	$2	purple	12.50	2.75
a		inverted overprint	—	650.00
QL84	$3	green	15.00	4.50
QL85	$4	grey	20.00	7.50
QL86	$5	blue	25.00	9.00
QL87	$10	violet brown	40.00	35.00
QL88	$20	red brown	95.00	75.00
QL89	$30	olive	75.00	20.00

1924
"BANKRUPTCY-LOI DE FAILLITE" Overprint
Perf. 11, 12

QL90	10¢	green	65.00	50.00
QL91	20¢	blue	7.50	2.75
a		hairlines	15.00	4.00
b		bluish paper	—	3.50
QL92	40¢	brown	7.50	3.50
QL93	50¢	black	12.50	3.75
a		hairlines	50.00	5.00
QL94	$1	red (shades)	15.00	5.00
a		orange	15.00	5.00
QL95	$2	purple	20.00	6.00
a		inverted overprint	—	650.00
b		hairlines	25.00	—

			Uncan.	Used
QL109	10¢	green & black	7.50	7.50
QL110	20¢	green & black	5.00	5.00
QL111	30¢	green & black	5.00	5.00
QL112	40¢	green & black	5.00	5.00
QL113	50¢	green & black	5.00	5.00
QL114	80¢	green & black	10.00	7.50
QL115	$1	green & black	300.00	300.00
QL116	$2	green & black	25.00	20.00

Uncan.   Used

QL91   QL94

QL96	$3	green	55.00	50.00
QL97	$4	grey	45.00	25.00
QL98	$5	blue	55.00	55.00
QL99	$10	brown	85.00	85.00

QL117   QL118

Overprinted "HONORAIRES-FEES"

QL117	$1	green & black	50.00	—

"BANKRUPTCY ACT-LOI DE FAILLITE" Overprnt

QL118	50¢	green & black	50.00	—
QL119	$1	green & black	175.00	—
QL120	$5	green & black	125.00	—

1924
"LOI DE FAILLITE-BANKRUPTCY ACT" Overprnt
Perf. 11, 12

QL102   QL106

QL100	10¢	green	—	75.00
QL101	20¢	blue	—	30.00
QL102	40¢	brown	—	40.00
QL103	50¢	black	—	90.00
QL104	$1	orange	—	30.00
QL105	$2	purple	—	50.00
QL106	$3	green	125.00	45.00
QL107	$4	grey	—	70.00
QL108	$5	blue	—	150.00

REGISTRATION STAMPS
1866 Lower Canada
Perf. 12

QR1   QR3a

QR1	5¢	red brown	5.00	3.00
	a	vermilion	3.00	1.50
QR2	15¢	red brown	5.00	3.00
	a	vermilion	4.00	2.00
QR3	30¢	red brown	25.00	15.00
	a	vermilion	6.00	4.00

Coat of Arms Issue
Perf. 10¾

QL109   QL116

1871 Beavers
Perf. 11½, 12, 12½, 11½ x 12 and 12 x 11½

QR4	2¢	green	75.00	60.00
QR5	5¢	green	2.00	0.25
QR6	15¢	green	2.00	0.25
	a	watermarked	—	—
QR7	30¢	green	10.00	0.35
	a	watermarked	—	50.00

			Uncan.	Used

	QR4		QR12	
QR8	30¢	blue	7.50	0.75
QR9	50¢	green	10.00	6.50
a		watermarked	—	55.00
QR10	50¢	black	6.00	4.00
a		watermarked	—	75.00
QR11	$1	orange	6.50	0.85
QR12	$1	carmine	10.00	7.50
QR13	$2	orange	12.50	4.50
QR14	$2	brown	12.50	3.00
a		watermarked	—	75.00
QR15	$5	orange	50.00	20.00

1912 Registration
Perf. 11, 12

	QR16		QR22	
QR16	5¢	black	4.50	0.25
QR17	10¢	bistre	1.25	0.25
QR18	15¢	green	1.75	1.50
QR19	20¢	green	1.50	0.35
QR20	30¢	blue	2.50	0.25
QR21	50¢	brown	2.50	0.30
QR22	$l	olive green	4.00	0.50
QR23	$2	red brown	4.50	0.50
QR24	$5	brown	12.50	2.00
QR25	$5	purple	12.50	3.00
QR26	$20	yellow	35.00	17.50
QR27	$50	orange	75.00	65.00
QR28	$100	carmine	100.00	50.00

Same design, but "LTD" added and larger type imprint at bottom

	QR29			
QR29	$2	brown	6.00	1.25

			Uncan.	Used

Coat of Arms Issue
Perf. 10¾

	QR30		QR35	
QR30	10¢	brown & black	7.50	5.00
QR31	20¢	brown & black	7.50	15.00
QR32	30¢	brown & black	9.00	5.00
QR33	50¢	brown & black	9.00	5.00
QR34	$1	brown & black	10.00	5.00
QR35	$2	brown & black	20.00	10.00
QR36	$5	brown & black	40.00	10.00
QR37		value omitted	325.00	—

This issue was followed by the use of meters in 1967.

LICENSE STAMPS
1876 Assurance.
Perf. 12, 12 x 11½

	QA3		QA11	
QA1	1¢	green	7.00	5.50
QA2	2¢	green	10.00	5.50
QA3	3¢	green	7.50	5.50
QA4	4¢	green	10.00	7.00
QA5	5¢	green	7.00	5.50
QA6	10¢	green	8.50	7.00
QA7	20¢	green	15.00	7.00
QA8	30¢	green	15.00	9.00
QA9	40¢	green	30.00	20.00
QA10	50¢	green	35.00	20.00
QA11	$1	violet	75.00	50.00
QA12	$2	violet	375.00	375.00
QA13	$3	violet	375.00	375.00
QA14	$4	violet	375.00	375.00
QA15	$5	violet	375.00	375.00

	Uncan.	Used

1889-1906 License stamps
Perf. 12

QA16   QA17

QA18

QA16	$2	brown	10.00	0.75
QA17	$7	green	50.00	40.00
QA18	$25	red	175.00	15.00

1893-1912 Law Stamps
With rubber stamped overprint "LICENSES"

QA20b   QA21

QA19		red o/p on QL51	—	15.00
a		purple o/p on QL51	—	7.50
QA20		red o/p on QL52	—	17.50
a		black o/p on QL52	25.00	7.50
b		purple o/p on QL52	—	7.50
QA21		red o/p on QL69	—	9.00
a		purple o/p on QL69	—	9.00

	Uncan.	Used

STOCK TRANSFER TAX STAMPS
1907 English Inscription
Perf. 12

QST1   QST6

QST1	2¢	blue	4.00	3.00
a		vert.pr.imperf betwn	—	875.00
QST2	10¢	carmine	5.00	4.00
QST3	20¢	black	27.50	25.00
QST4	50¢	yellow	25.00	20.00
QST5	$1	red	17.50	15.00
QST6	$2	brown	35.00	35.00
QST7	$10	purple	700.00	700.00
QST8	$30	green	—	700.00

1913 English & French inscription

QST9   QST15

QST9	1¢	violet	3.50	3.50
QST10	2¢	blue	1.00	0.25
QST11	3¢	carmine	1.50	1.50
QST12	10¢	olive	1.50	0.25
QST13	20¢	slate	2.00	0.35
QST14	50¢	buff	4.50	0.50
QST15	$1	red	6.00	0.50
QST16	$2	brown	10.00	0.50
QST17	$10	purple	35.00	15.00
QST18	$30	green	75.00	35.00

PROHIBITION STAMPS
1919 Prohibition
Perf. 11, 12

QP1	1¢	orange	12.50	7.50
QP2	2¢	blue	3.50	3.50
QP3	5¢	light brown	5.00	4.50
QP4	10¢	bistre brown	25.00	25.00
QP5	10¢	black	6.00	6.00
QP6	20¢	vermilion	17.50	15.00
QP7	50¢	dark brown	35.00	35.00
QP8	$1	olive green	55.00	50.00
QP9	$5	blue green	350.00	350.00
QP10	$10	blue violet	350.00	350.00

Uncan.   Used

QP10

			Uncan.	Used
QV1	1¢	ochre	1.00	1.00
QV2	2¢	red	1.25	1.25
QV3	5¢	orange	2.00	1.75
QV4	10¢	grey black	3.50	3.00
QV5	25¢	brown	7.50	6.00
QV6	50¢	green	15.00	12.50
QV7	$1	blue	20.00	20.00
QV8	$2	purple	25.00	25.00
QV9	$5	yellow green	35.00	35.00

Complete set handstamped "SPECIMEN" in blue $75

UNEMPLOYMENT RELIEF TAX
1934-39

QU1

QU3

QU1	5¢	orange	1.00	0.25
QU2	10¢	olive green	1.50	0.50
QU3	15¢	violet	1.25	0.45

Various forgeries to defraud the Quebec government were made by bootleggers

TEMPORARY VACATION PAY STAMPS

QV11			QV15	
QV10	1¢	ochre	75.00	75.00
QV11	2¢	red orange	75.00	—
QV12	5¢	orange	75.00	—
QV13	25¢	brown	55.00	—
QV14	50¢	green	55.00	—
QV15	$1	blue	60.00	—

SAVINGS STAMPS
LA CAISSE POPULAIRE
Desjardins issue
Perf. 12

QCP1		QCP4	QCP6	
QCP1	1¢	red	10.00	10.00
QCP2	5¢	blue	10.00	10.00
a		imperf pair	125.00	—
QCP3	10¢	brown	75.00	75.00
QCP4	25¢	green	10.00	10.00

Jacques Cartier issue
Perf. 12

QCP5	1¢	red	20.00	—
QCP6	5¢	blue	20.00	—

VACATION PAY STAMPS
1958 Vacation Pay
Perf. 12

QV1   QV7

QUEBEC FISH & GAME
QFG1		pink on green	50.00	—

PROVINCE OF SASKATCHEWAN

Uncan. Used   Uncan. Used

LAW STAMPS
1907 Coat of Arms
First printing. Sheets of 25

The words "Cents" or "Dollars" 2mm above bottom frame line. The $1 value reads "Dollars". The scroll background is green on most values.

SL1

SL1a

SL7

SL15

SL18a

			Uncan.	Used
SL1	5¢	blue on white	15.00	10.00
a		inverted centre	—	750.00
SL2	10¢	violet on pink	15.00	8.00
SL3	20¢	black on blue	25.00	15.00
SL4	25¢	brown on green	30.00	7.50
SL5	50¢	green on yellow	35.00	9.00
SL6	75¢	black on red	50.00	10.00
SL7	$1	brown on white	100.00	75.00
SL8	$2	purple on pink	120.00	90.00
SL9	$3	brown on blue	145.00	100.00
SL10	$5	black on green	500.00	450.00
SL11	$10	brown on yellow	500.00	450.00
SL12	$20	black on red	500.00	450.00

1907
Second Printing

The words "Cents" or "Dollars" are 1 mm above the bottom frame line. The $1 value reads "Dollar".

			Uncan.	Used
SL13	5¢	blue on white	25.00	10.00
a		vert.pr. impf.horiz.	—	—
SL14	10¢	violet on pink	20.00	4.00
SL15	25¢	brown on green	20.00	4.00
SL16	50¢	green on yellow	20.00	7.00
SL17	75¢	black on red	20.00	6.00
a		double overprint	—	175.00
b		"Ccnts" error	—	500.00
SL18	$1	brown on white	75.00	25.00
a		inverted background	50.00	7.50
SL19	$2	purple on pink	60.00	8.00
a		doubled purple	—	250.00
SL20	$3	brown on blue	75.00	7.50

1907
Type set in black on green background, perf. 12

SL21

SL27

			Uncan.	Used
SL21	5¢	black	25.00	15.00
SL22	10¢	black	25.00	7.00
SL23	20¢	black	145.00	125.00
SL24	25¢	black	25.00	5.00
SL25	50¢	black	25.00	5.00
SL26	75¢	black	25.00	10.00
SL27	$1	black	30.00	12.00
SL28	$2	black	30.00	17.50
SL29	$3	black	65.00	50.00
SL30	$5	black	500.00	450.00
SL31	$10	black	450.00	375.00
SL32	$20	black	450.00	375.00

1908 Law Stamps
Perf. 12, engraved

SL34

SL42

			Uncan.	Used
SL33	5¢	blue	7.50	5.00
SL34	10¢	lake	3.50	0.50
SL35	20¢	olive green	5.00	1.25
SL36	25¢	lilac	5.00	0.45
SL37	50¢	orange	5.00	0.60
SL38	75¢	yellow brown	5.00	1.00
SL39	$1	black brown	6.00	0.50
SL40	$2	brown	7.50	1.25
SL41	$3	slate	15.00	1.00
SL42	$5	blue green	17.50	2.00
SL43	$10	brown	30.00	5.00
SL44	$20	indian red	55.00	12.50

1938 Law Stamps
Perf. 12, engraved

	SL45		SL50	
SL45	5¢	sepia	7.50	6.00
SL46	10¢	orange	5.00	4.00
SL47	20¢	slate	25.00	20.00
SL48	25¢	light blue	2.50	0.50
SL49	50¢	olive green	2.75	0.50
SL50	75¢	orange	3.50	1.25
SL51	$1	blue	3.50	0.60
SL52	$2	purple	5.00	2.00
SL53	$3	olive yellow	7.50	2.00
SL54	$5	brown	12.50	3.50
SL55	$10	green	25.00	7.50
SL56	$20	rose carmine	60.00	55.00

Without "AMERICAN BANK NOTE CO. OTTAWA" imprint at bottom.

	SL57		SL63	
SL57	5¢	sepia	1.00	—
SL58	10¢	red	1.00	—
SL59	25¢	blue	1.50	—
SL60	50¢	olive green	2.00	—
SL61	$1	blue	3.00	—
SL62	$2	purple	6.00	—

			Uncan.	Used
SL63	$3	ochre	9.00	—
SL64	$5	brown	15.00	—
SL65	$10	green	30.00	—
SL66	$20	rose	65.00	—
SL67	$50	blue	125.00	—

Same design, but rouletted

	SL76		SL77	
SL68	5¢	sepia	0.25	—
SL69	10¢	dull vermilion	0.25	—
SL70	25¢	blue	0.25	—
SL71	50¢	olive green	0.50	—
SL72	$1	blue	1.00	—
a		double print	500.00	—
SL73	$2	deep lilac	2.00	—
SL74	$3	ochre	3.00	—
SL75	$5	sepia	5.00	—
SL76	$10	green	10.00	—
SL77	$20	rose carmine	20.00	—
SL78	$50	blue	50.00	—

Overprints on SL57/78 were done privately. They are cinderellas.

SASKATOON ELECTRICAL INSPECTION
1911
Type set, rouletted

	SE1			
SE1	25¢	dull red	375.00	—
a		inverted border	450.00	—

1913
Lithographed, perf. 12

SE2	50¢	blue	400.00	—

Uncan. Used   Uncan. Used

SE2

SE7

1929.
Lithographed, red serial number without letter.
Perf. 12

1927
Lithographed, perf. 12. Issued without gum

SE4

SE5

			Uncan.	Used
SE3	25¢	scarlet	450.00	—
SE4	50¢	scarlet	350.00	—
a		bisect on document	—	450.00
SE5	$1	scarlet	350.00	—

SE9

SE11

			Uncan.	Used
SE9	25¢	black & green	6.00	3.50
a		pinperf	—	50.00
SE10	50¢	black & blue	15.00	3.50
a		pinperf	—	50.00
SE11	$1	black & pink	—	3.50

SASKATCHEWAN ELECTRICAL INSPECTION
1929
Typographed in black on coloured paper.
Perf. 11

			Uncan.	Used
SE6	25¢	pale green paper	7.50	5.00
SE7	50¢	blue paper	—	4.00
SE8	$1	red paper	—	4.00

SE6-8 are always perfin cancelled "P.S." province of Saskatchewan.

1937-47
Control number with letter "A-D", lithographed

SE14

SE26

			Uncan.	Used
SE12	1¢	yellow "C"	4.50	3.00
a		double print	—	50.00
SE13	5¢	grey "C"	6.00	5.00
a		double print	—	50.00
SE14	5¢	grey "D"	4.00	3.50
a		pinperf	35.00	—
SE15	10¢	orange "C"	4.00	3.00
a		double print	—	50.00
SE16	10¢	orange "D"	4.00	3.00
a		pinperf	—	25.00
SE17	25¢	green "B"	5.00	3.50
a		pinperf	—	25.00
SE18	25¢	green "C"	6.00	4.50
a		double print	55.00	50.00
SE19	50¢	blue "B"	—	4.00
a		pinperf	—	50.00
SE20	50¢	blue "C"	6.00	5.00
a		double black print	60.00	50.00

SE6

			Uncan.	Used
SE21	50¢	blue "D", 4mm #	5.00	4.50
a		5 mm control number	8.00	6.00
b		pinperf, 4 mm #	—	25.00
SE22	$1	pink "B"	—	3.50
a		pinperf	—	25.00
SE23	$1	pink "C"	—	5.00
a		double black print	60.00	50.00
SE24	$1	pink, 4mm # "D"	5.00	4.00
a	$1	pink, 5mm # "D"	—	7.00
SE25	$2	violet, 4mm # "A"	10.00	9.00
a	$2	violet, 5mm #	—	12.50
SE26	$5	buff "C"	12.00	8.00
a		double print	—	100.00
SE27	$10	purple, 5mm controls	25.00	10.00
a		4mm control numbers	25.00	10.00

1947
Handstamped overprints in blue on SE27, SE27a

	SE28		SE30	
SE28	10¢	on $10 (SE27a)	7.00	7.00
SE29	25¢	on $10 (SE27)	9.00	7.50
a		doubled overprint	—	—
SE30	50¢	on $10 (SE27a)	25.00	20.00

SASKATCHEWAN TELEPHONE CO.
1900.
Issued without gum. Printed in black on colored paper, value overprinted in red

ST3

ST1	10¢	light yellow	1500.	—
ST2	15¢	blue paper	1500.	—
ST3	25¢	rose paper	1500.	—
ST4	50¢	dark yellow	1500.	—
ST5	$1	white paper	1500.	—

1909-49 Small Size Franks
Printed in booklet panes of 20. Issued without gum

ST6   ST7

			Uncan.	Used
ST6	5¢	orange	25.00	25.00
b		booklet pane of 20	600.00	—
ST7	25¢	green	25.00	25.00
a		watermarked	50.00	—
b		booklet pane of 20	600.00	—

1911 Series

ST8   ST9

"C" control letter issued without gum

ST8	5¢	gray black	3.50	3.50
a		watermarked	7.50	7.50
b		booklet pane of 20	100.00	—
c		pane perfed at right	150.00	—
d		pane perf at left	150.00	—
ST9	25¢	blue	4.00	4.00
a		watermarked	10.00	10.00
b		booklet pane of 20	250.00	—

1919
No control letter, 1½ mm control numbers. Series 1 - 500. Issued without gum

ST10   ST11

ST10	5¢	grey black	2.50	—
a		watermarked	4.50	—
b		double print	35.00	—
c		booklet pane of 20	75.00	—
ST11	25¢	grey black	2.50	—
a		watermarked	4.50	—
b		double print	35.00	—
c		booklet pane of 20	75.00	—

1932
2½ mm control numbers, no control letter. Series 501-800. Issued without gum

ST12   ST13

ST12	5¢	grey black	2.00	—
ST12	a	watermarked	4.00	—
ST12	b	booklet pane of 20	50.00	—
ST13	25¢	grey black	2.00	—
a		watermarked	4.00	—
b		booklet pane of 20	50.00	—

		Uncan.	Used

1949 Re-drawn

2½ mm control numbers, no control letter.
Series 801-999. Issued without gum

ST14   ST15

			Uncan.	Used
ST14	5¢	black	2.50	—
	a	watermarked	4.50	—
	b	complete pane of 20	50.00	—
	c	error pane with diff. #'s	150.00	—
	d	major plate scratch	15.00	—
	e	strip of 5 incl. imperf pair	750.00	—
ST15	25¢	black	2.50	—
	a	watermarked	4.50	—
	b	complete pane of 20	50.00	—

YUKON TERRITORY

1903 Dawson Mining Court

YL1   YL4

YL1	10¢	vermilion	85.00	85.00
YL2	25¢	vermilion	50.00	20.00
YL3	50¢	vermilion	60.00	40.00
YL4	$1	vermilion	75.00	50.00
YL5	$2	vermilion	100.00	60.00
YL6	$3	vermilion	150.00	75.00

1903 Territorial Court

YL8   YL10

YL7	10¢	blue	30.00	17.50
YL8	25¢	blue	17.50	2.50
YL9	50¢	blue	15.00	2.50
YL10	$1	blue	17.50	3.50
YL11	$2	blue	17.50	4.50
YL12	$3	blue	25.00	10.00

Overprints on 1903 issue

Overprint color as noted

YL13   YL14

			Uncan.	Used
YL13	25¢	on 10c silver o/p	75.00	25.00
	a	double overprint	300.00	300.00
YL14	$1	blue o/p on 50¢	75.00	60.00
	a	purplish blue o/p	75.00	60.00
YL15	$2	black o/p on 50¢	75.00	65.00
	a	double overprint	—	850.00
YL16	$3	black o/p on 50¢	120.00	110.00
YL17	$5	black o/p on 50¢	125.00	110.00
YL18	$5	blue o/p on 50¢	85.00	75.00
YL19	$20	black o/p on 50¢	325.00	300.00
	a	double overprint	—	500.00
	b	manuscript "$20"	—	500.00

TELEPHONE & TELEGRAPH FRANKS

			Uncan.	Used

Canadian Pacific Railways;
Issued in booklet panes of 4.
8 panes per book. perf. 11, 12, 12½

TCP2

			Uncan.	Used
TCP1	1887	black	15.00	—
TCP2	1889	black	15.00	—
TCP3	1890	black	15.00	—
TCP4	1891	black	15.00	—
TCP5	1892	black	12.50	—
TCP6	1893	black	9.00	—
TCP7	1894	black	9.00	—
TCP8	1895	black	9.00	—
TCP9	1896	black	9.00	—
TCP10	1897	black	9.00	—
a		watermarked	35.00	—
TCP11	1898	black	15.00	—
TCP12	1899	black	9.00	—
TCP13	1900	black	9.00	—
TCP14	1901	black	9.00	—
TCP15	1902	blue	15.00	—
TCP16	1903	brown	17.50	—
TCP17	1904	slate	20.00	—
TCP18	1905	black	10.00	—
TCP19	1906	black	20.00	—
TCP20	1907	black	15.00	—
TCP21	1908	black	10.00	—
a		watermarked	35.00	—
TCP22	1909	black	12.50	—
a		watermarked	45.00	—
TCP23	1910	black	12.50	—
a		watermarked	35.00	—
TCP24	1911	black	12.50	—
a		watermarked	35.00	—
TCP25	1912	black	12.50	—
a		hor. pair, imperf between	300.00	—
TCP26	1913	slate	75.00	—
a		watermarked	100.00	—
b		very thin paper	150.00	—
TCP27	1914	black	45.00	—
a		watermarked	75.00	—
TCP28	1915	black	35.00	—
a		watermarked	45.00	—
TCP29	1916	black	15.00	—
TCP30	1917	black	25.00	—
TCP31	1918	black	17.50	—
TCP32	1919	black	35.00	—
TCP33	1920	black	45.00	—
TCP34	1921	black	17.50	—
TCP35	1922	black	25.00	—
TCP36	1923	black	25.00	—
a		bottom double print	150.00	—
TCP37	1924	black	17.50	—
TCP38	1925	black	15.00	—
TCP39	1926	black	10.00	—
TCP40	1927	black	15.00	—

TCP47

			Uncan.	Used
TCP41	1928	black	17.50	—
TCP42	1929	black	25.00	—
TCP43	1930	black	35.00	—
TCP44	1931	black	45.00	—
TCP45	1932	black	90.00	—
TCP46	1933	black	45.00	—
TCP47	1934	black	45.00	—
TCP48	1935	black	60.00	—
TCP49	1936	black	75.00	—

Great North Western Telegraph Co.

	TGN1		TGN21	
TGN1	1890	blue	25.00	—
TGN2	1891	red	30.00	—
TGN3	1892	olive green	30.00	—
TGN4	1893	brown	75.00	—
TGN5	1894	slate	25.00	—
TGN6	1895	violet	25.00	—
TGN7	1896	red	25.00	—
TGN8	1897	blue	15.00	—
TGN9	1898	green	15.00	—
TGN10	1899	lilac	20.00	—
TGN11	1900	red	15.00	—
TGN12	1901	blue green	15.00	—
TGN13	1902	black	15.00	—
TGN14	1903	lilac	15.00	—
TGN15	1904	blue	10.00	—
TGN16	1905	red	20.00	—
TGN17	1906	green	15.00	—
TGN18	1907	plum	15.00	—
TGN19	1908	purple	10.00	—
TGN20	1909	blue	10.00	—
TGN21	1910	red	15.00	—
TGN22	1911	black	10.00	—
TGN23	1912	black	10.00	—
TGN24	1913	blue	15.00	—
TGN25	1914	black	10.00	—
TGN26	1915	green	15.00	—
TGN27	1916	black	12.50	—
TGN28	1917	blue	12.50	—

			Uncan.	Used
TGN29	1918	slate	15.00	—
TGN30	1919	black	17.50	—
TGN31	1920	black	15.00	—

Algoma Central Railway

TAC1	1890	dark blue	2500.	—
TAC2	1902	black on blue, red #	2500.	—

Dominion De Forest Telegraph Co

TDF1	1906	blue	3000.	—

Canadian Northern Telegraph Co.

TNR2

TNR1	1904	light blue	600.00	—
TNR2	1905	blue	600.00	—
TNR3	1906	blue	600.00	—
TNR4	1907	blue	600.00	—
TNR5	1908	blue	500.00	—
TNR6	1909	black	500.00	—

TNR7

TNR7	1910	black	500.00	—
TNR8	1911	black	500.00	—
TNR9	1912	black	325.00	—
TNR10	1913	black	500.00	—
TNR11	1914	black	500.00	—

Grand Trunk Pacific Railways

TGT1	1911	black	500.00	—
TGT2	1912	green	450.00	—
TGT3	1913	ultramarine	500.00	—
TGT4	1914	grey	225.00	250.00
TGT5	1915	black	600.00	—
TGT6	1916	black	275.00	—
	a	re-entry	300.00	—
TGT7	1917	black	275.00	—
TGT8	1918	black	200.00	—

			Uncan.	Used

TGT2			TGT10	
TGT9	1919	grey	275.00	—
TGT10	1920	black	125.00	—

Canadian National Railways

TCN2

TCN1	1921	black	15.00	—
TCN2	1922	red	10.00	—
TCN3	1923	green	25.00	—
TCN4	1923	unshaded	1000.	—

	TCN5		TCN10	
TCN5	1925-26	blue	10.00	—
TCN6	1927-28	blue	30.00	—
TCN7	1929-30	blue	10.00	—
TCN8	1931-32	black	125.00	—
TCN9	1933-34	black	75.00	—
TCN10	1935	black	45.00	—

				Uncan.	Used

Bell Telephone Company
Messenger service
No date

TBT1

			Uncan.	Used
TBT1		black, no value	175.00	—

1900-07
Perf. 11, 11½, 12, 14.
All are uncancelled issued in booklet panes of 5

TBT2	1900	10¢	black on yellow	35.00	—

TBT5

TBT3		15¢	black on blue	35.00	—
a			watermarked	40.00	—
TBT4		25¢	black on white	35.00	—
a			watermarked	45.00	—
TBT5	1901	10¢	black on yellow	35.00	—
a			watermarked	45.00	—
TBT6		15¢	black on green	35.00	—
TBT7		25¢	black on white	40.00	—
TBT8	1902	10¢	black on yellow	40.00	—
a			watermarked	50.00	—
TBT9		15¢	black on blue	45.00	—
a			watermarked	50.00	—
TBT10		25¢	black on white	40.00	—
a			watermarked	45.00	—
TBT11	1903	10¢	black on pink	40.00	—
a			re-entry, watermark	75.00	—
TBT12		15¢	black on blue	40.00	—
a			watermarked	45.00	—
b			re-entry	50.00	—
TBT13		25¢	black on white	40.00	—
a			watermarked	45.00	—
TBT14	1904	10¢	black on pink	40.00	—
a			watermarked	50.00	—
TBT15		15¢	black on blue	27.50	—
a			watermarked	50.00	—
TBT16		25¢	black on white	30.00	—
a			watermarked	45.00	—
TBT17	1905	10¢	black on pink	40.00	—
a			watermarked	50.00	—

TBT18

TBT18		15¢	black on blue	37.50	—
a			watermarked	50.00	—
b			re-entry	75.00	—
TBT19		25¢	black on white	37.50	—
a			watermarked	45.00	—
TBT20	1906	10¢	black on pink	40.00	—
TBT21		15¢	black on blue	40.00	—
a			watermarked	45.00	—
TBT22		25¢	black on white	50.00	—
TBT23	1907	10¢	black on pink	55.00	—
TBT24		15¢	black on blue	55.00	—
a			watermarked	60.00	—
TBT25		25¢	black on white	55.00	—
a			watermarked	60.00	—

Perf. 11, 11½, 12, 14, rouletted.
Issued in booklet panes of 20.
Watermarked copies add 50% premium

TBT31

TBT42

TBT26	1907	5¢	red	50.00	—
a			watermarked	120.00	—
TBT27		5¢	green	100.00	—
TBT28		25¢	blue	50.00	—
TBT29		25¢	plum	50.00	—
a			watermarked	110.00	—
TBT30	1908	5¢	red	25.00	—
TBT31		5¢	green	25.00	—
TBT32		25¢	black	25.00	—
TBT33		25¢	blue	25.00	—
TBT34		25¢	purple brown	25.00	—
TBT35	1909	5¢	red	35.00	—
TBT36		5¢	yellow orange	25.00	—
TBT37		5¢	green	25.00	—
TBT38		25¢	black	25.00	—
a			watermarked	50.00	—
TBT39		25¢	blue	30.00	—
TBT40		25¢	purple brown	30.00	—
TBT41	1910	5¢	yellow orange	30.00	—
TBT42		5¢	red	2.00	—
TBT43		5¢	green	25.00	—
TBT44		25¢	black	25.00	—
TBT45		25¢	blue	3.00	—
TBT46		25¢	purple brown	25.00	—
TBT47	1911	5¢	yellow orange	15.00	—

TBT49

TBT60

TBT48		5¢	red	15.00	—
TBT49		5¢	green	1.50	—
TBT50		25¢	black	35.00	—
TBT51		25¢	blue	15.00	—
TBT52		25¢	purple brown	1.50	—
TBT53	1912	5¢	yellow orange	0.75	—
TBT54		5¢	green	25.00	—

TBT74

TBT77

TBT119

				Uncan.	Used					Uncan.	Used
TBT55		25¢	blue	0.75	—	TBT107	1937	5¢	orange	4.00	—
TBT56		25¢	purple brown	25.00	—	a			"telephole" error	25.00	—
TBT57	1913	5¢	yellow orange	0.75	—	TBT108		25¢	blue	8.00	—
TBT58		5¢	green	5.00	—	TBT109	1938	5¢	pale orange	25.00	—
TBT59		25¢	blue	1.00	—	a			"telephole" error	45.00	—
TBT60		25¢	purple brown	3.50	—	TBT110		25¢	blue	7.50	—
TBT61	1914	5¢	yellow orange	2.50	—	TBT111	1939	5¢	orange	1.25	—
TBT62		25¢	blue	2.50	—	a			"telephole" error	25.00	—
TBT63	1915	5¢	yellow orange	0.75	—	TBT112		25¢	blue	1.25	—
TBT64		25¢	blue	2.00	—	TBT113	1940	5¢	orange	1.25	—
a			"telephoke" error	25.00	—	a			"telephole" error	25.00	—
TBT65	1916	5¢	yellow orange	0.75	—	TBT114		25¢	blue	2.00	—
TBT66		25¢	blue	2.00	—	a			plate scratch	10.00	—
TBT67	1917	5¢	yellow orange	5.00	—	TBT115	1941	5¢	orange	4.00	—
TBT68		25¢	blue	5.00	—	a			"telephole" error	25.00	—
TBT69	1918	5¢	yellow	5.00	—	TBT116		25¢	blue	15.00	—
TBT70		25¢	blue	5.00	—	TBT117	1942	5¢	orange	1.25	—
TBT71	1919	5¢	yellow	0.75	—	a			"telephole" error	25.00	—
TBT72		25¢	blue	0.75	—	TBT118		25¢	blue	1.25	—
TBT73	1920	5¢	yellow orange	0.75	—	a			plate scratch	10.00	—
a		5¢	yellow	10.00	—	TBT119	1943	5¢	orange	1.25	—
TBT74		25¢	blue	0.75	—	a			"telephole" error	25.00	—
TBT75	1921	5¢	lemon	5.00	—	TBT120		25¢	blue	7.50	—
TBT76		25¢	blue	5.00	—	TBT121	1944	5¢	orange	1.25	—
TBT77	1922	5¢	yellow	10.00	—	a			"telephole" error	25.00	—
TBT78		25¢	blue	10.00	—	TBT122		25¢	blue	1.25	—
TBT79	1923	5¢	yellow	1.50	—	TBT123	1945	5¢	orange	1.25	—
TBT80		25¢	blue	1.50	—	a			"telephole" error	25.00	—
TBT81	1924	5¢	yellow	1.00	—	TBT124		25¢	blue	1.25	—
TBT82		25¢	blue	1.00	—	TBT125	1946	5¢	yellow	1.25	—
TBT83	1925	5¢	yellow	7.50	—	a			"telephole" error	25.00	—
TBT84		25¢	blue	7.50	—	TBT126		25¢	blue	1.25	—
TBT85	1926	5¢	yellow	5.00	—	TBT127	1947	5¢	yellow	1.25	—
TBT86		25¢	blue	5.00	—	a			"telephole" error	25.00	—
TBT87	1927	5¢	yellow	2.00	—	TBT128		25¢	blue	1.25	—
TBT88		25¢	blue	1.50	—	TBT129	1948	5¢	yellow	1.25	—
TBT89	1928	5¢	yellow	0.75	—	a			"telephole" error	25.00	—
TBT90		25¢	blue	0.75	—	TBT130		25¢	blue	1.25	—
TBT91	1929	5¢	yellow	2.00	—	a			plate scratch	10.00	—
TBT92		25¢	blue	2.00	—	TBT131	1949	5¢	yellow	1.25	—
TBT93	1930	5¢	yellow	1.50	—	a			"telephole" error	25.00	—
TBT94		25¢	blue	1.50	—	TBT132		25¢	blue	1.25	—
a			plate scratch	10.00	—	TBT133	1950	5¢	yellow	1.25	—
TBT95	1931	5¢	yellow	0.75	—	a			"telephole" error	25.00	—
TBT96		25¢	blue	0.75	—	TBT134		25¢	blue	1.25	—
a			plate scratch	10.00	—	TBT135	1951	5¢	yellow	1.00	—
TBT97	1932	5¢	yellow	1.50	—	a			"telephole" error	25.00	—
TBT98		25¢	blue	2.00	—	TBT136		25¢	blue	1.25	—
a			plate scratch	10.00	—	TBT137	1952	5¢	yellow	1.00	—
TBT99	1933	5¢	red orange	7.50	—	a			"telephole" error	25.00	—
TBT100		25¢	blue	7.50	—	TBT138		25¢	blue	1.25	—
TBT101	1934	5¢	yellow orange	5.00	—	TBT139	1953	5¢	yellow	1.00	—
a			"934" date error	50.00	—	a			"telephole" error	25.00	—
TBT102		25¢	blue	5.00	—	TBT140		25¢	blue	1.50	—
a			plate scratch	10.00	—	a			plate scratch	10.00	—
TBT103	1935	5¢	red orange	2.00	—	TBT141	1954	5¢	yellow	1.00	—
a			"telephole" error	25.00	—	a			"telephole" error	25.00	—
TBT104		25¢	blue	4.00	—	b			plate scratch	10.00	—
TBT105	1936	5¢	orange	4.00	—	TBT142		25¢	blue	1.25	—
a			"telephoie" error	25.00	—	TBT143	1955	5¢	yellow	1.00	—
TBT106		25¢	blue	6.00	—	a			"telephole" error	25.00	—

				Uncan.	Used
TBT144		25¢	blue	1.25	—
TBT145	1956	5¢	yellow	1.00	—
a			"telephoie" error	25.00	—
TBT146		25¢	blue	1.25	—
TBT147	1957	5¢	yellow	1.50	—
a			"telephoie" error	25.00	—
TBT148		25¢	blue	1.25	—
a			plate scratch	10.00	—

				Uncan.	Used
TBT149	1958	5¢	yellow	1.00	—
a			"telephoie" error	25.00	—
TBT150		25¢	blue	2.50	—
TBT151	1959	5¢	yellow	2.50	—
a			"telephoie" error	25.00	—
TBT152		25¢	blue	3.75	—

PRISONER OF WAR FRANKS

Used by prisoners of war interned in Canada during World War II these franks were valid for postage in Canada on parcels weighing up to 20 pounds. All stamps are black printing on red paper.

PWF1

PWF2

PWF3

PWF4

PWF5

PWF6

			Uncan.	Used
Imperf. no inscripton at top above Canada				
PWF1	1940	"P/W" large type	175.00	225.00
PWF2	1941	"P/W" small type	150.00	200.00
Inscription at top above Canada				
PWF3	1943		150.00	175.00

			Uncan.	Used
Rouletted, inscription at top above Canada				
PWF4	1944		125.00	165.00
a		complete pane of 5	675.00	—
PWF5	1945		275.00	300.00
a		complete pane of 5	1,550.	—
PWF6	1946		20.00	45.00
a		complete pane of 5	115.00	—

HAMILTON SAVINGS BANK

OHB1　　　OHB3　　　OHB4

			Uncan.	Used
ca. 1890, perf. 12½				
OHB1	1¢	yellow orange	—	35.00
OHB2	1¢	grey lilac	—	55.00
OHB3	5¢	blue	—	35.00
OHB4	25¢	red	—	35.00

PRAIRIE PROVINCES CONSERVATION STAMPS

PC1　　　　　　PC2　　　　　　　　PC3

PC4　　　　　　　　　PC6

			Uncan.	Used
1942				
Issued in sheets of 20.				
Designed by Dr. W. Rowan				
PC1	25¢	brown + black, pheasant	7.50	—
PC2	25¢	green, mallard duck	12.50	—
PC3	25¢	purple, partridge	7.50	—
PC4	25¢	blue, Canada goose	12.50	—
a		double print	125.00	—
PC5	25¢	red & brown, grouse	7.50	—

			Uncan.	Used
1943				
Issued in pane of 5				
PC6	25¢	blue + red, partridge	35.00	—
a		complete pane of 5	200.00	—

ALBERTA WILDLIFE CERTIFICATE STAMPS

These Alberta hunting stamps have been issued since 1964. Prior to 1970 the stamps bore no date, but show a date from 1970 on. Albertans were charged a lower rate than non-residents and there are separate stamps for each residency category with details changing from year to year. Since 1972 a special resource development tax stamp has been printed directly onto the wildlife certificate and other stamps were added as needed. No mint stamps exist as all unsold stamps were destroyed at the end of each year. Details on many of these stamps are sparce and any additional information and stamps will be welcomed. Pricing will be established as more of these come onto the market.

Face Value		Description

1964 RESIDENT

Perf. 12½, size 25 x 38 mm
Background: Lake & forest scene.
First background colour, then lettering colour.

AW1	2.50	BIRD GAME, blue, blue
AW2	5.00	BIG GAME, pink, red
AW3	—	ANTELOPE
AW4	5.00	SPRING BEAR, pale pinkish buff, brn
a	—	light double print
AW5	2.00	MULE DEER, grey, black
AW6	2.00	WHITETAIL DEER, green, green
AW7	7.50	GOAT, light blue, dark blue
AW8	7.50	SHEEP, light yellow, brown

1964 NON-RESIDENT CANADIAN

AW9	50.00	BIG GAME, light yellow, brown

1964 NON-RESIDENT CANADIAN & ALIEN

AW10	25.00	SPRING BEAR
AW11	15.00	WHITETAIL DEER, light pink, dark pink

1964 NON-RESIDENT ALIEN

AW12	25.00	BIRD GAME
AW13	100.00	BIG GAME, light brown, dark brown
a	—	double print dark brown

1965 RESIDENT

Perf. 12½, size: 32 x 28 mm
Background similar to 1964 issue.

AW14	2.50	BIRD GAME, blue, dark blue
AW15	5.00	BIG GAME, pink, dark pink
AW16	5.00	SPRING BEAR, buff, brown
AW17	3.00	MULE DEER, grey, dark brown
AW18	3.00	WHITETAIL DEER, green, dark green
AW19	7.50	GOAT
AW20	7.50	SHEEP, yellow, yellow brown
AW21	2.00	DUPLICATE LICENSE

1965 NON-RESIDENT CANADIAN

Size: 41 x 35 mm (AW22-AW26)

AW22	50.00	BIG GAME

1965 NON-RESIDENT CANADIAN & ALIEN

AW23	25.00	SPRING BEAR, buff, brown
AW24	15.00	WHITETAIL DEER

1965 NON-RESIDENT ALIEN

AW25	25.00	BIRD GAME
AW26	100.00	BIG GAME, brown, dark brown

1965 SPECIAL LICENSE,

Size: 53 x 25 mm. Rouletted

AW27	7.50	ANTELOPE, white, dark blue

1966 RESIDENT

Dimensions & perfs. same as 1965

AW28	2.50	BIRD GAME, orange, dark orange
AW29	5.00	BIG GAME, green, dark green
AW30	5.00	SPRING BEAR
AW31	7.50	CARIBOU, olive, dark olive
AW32	3.00	MULE DEER, carmine, dark carmine
AW33	3.00	WHITETAIL DEER, pink, dark red
AW34	7.50	GOAT
AW35	7.50	TROPHY SHEEP, purple, dark purple
AW36	2.00	DUPLICATE LICENSE

1966 NON-RESIDENT CANADIAN

AW37	50.00	BIG GAME

1966 NON-RESIDENT CANADIAN & ALIEN

AW38	25.00	SPRING BEAR
AW39	15.00	WHITETAIL DEER

1966 NON-RESIDENT ALIEN

AW40	25.00	BIRD GAME
AW41	100.00	BIG GAME, yellow, yellow brown

1966 RESIDENT SPECIAL LICENSES

AW42	7.50	ANTELOPE, like AW27
AW43	3.00	WAINWRIGHT DEER
AW44	5.00	NON-TROPHY SHEEP

1967 RESIDENT

Dimensions & perfs. same as 1965

AW45	2.50	BIRD GAME, carmine, dark carmine
AW46	5.00	BIG GAME, pink, dark red
AW47	5.00	SPRING BEAR

	Face Value	Description
AW48	7.50	CARIBOU, blue, dark blue
AW49	3.00	MULE DEER, orange, dark orange
AW50	3.00	WHITETAIL DEER, green, dark green
AW51	7.50	GOAT
AW52	1.00	SAGE GROUSE
AW53	7.50	TROPHY SHEEP, grey & black
AW54	2.00	DUPLICATE LICENSE

1967 NON-RESIDENT CANADIAN

AW55	5.00	BIRD GAME, brown, dark brown
AW56	25.00	BIG GAME

1967 NON-RESIDENT CANADIAN & ALIEN

AW57	25.00	SPRING BEAR
AW58	15.00	WHITETAIL DEER
AW59	25.00	SPECIAL MOOSE, yellow

1967 NON-RESIDENT ALIEN

AW60	25.00	BIRD GAME, purple
AW61	150.00	BIG GAME, pink, green

1967 SPECIAL LICENSE

AW62	7.50	ANTELOPE, white, 26 x 53 mm
AW63	3.00	WAINWRIGHT DEER
AW64	5.00	NON-TROPHY SHEEP

1968 RESIDENT

Perf. 12½. Size: 37 x 32 mm
Background as before.

AW65	2.50	BIRD GAME, green, dark green
AW66	5.00	BLACK BEAR
AW67	7.50	GRIZZLY BEAR
AW68	7.50	CARIBOU, pink, red
AW69	3.00	MULE DEER, grey, black
AW70	3.00	WHITETAIL DEER, blue, dark blue
AW71	5.00	ELK, purple, dark purple
AW72	7.50	GOAT, yellow, brown yellow
AW73	5.00	MOOSE, buff, brown
AW74	5.00	MOOSE ZONE 1
AW75	7.50	TROPHY SHEEP, yellow, black
AW76	2.00	DUPLICATE LICENSE

1968 NON-RESIDENT CANADIAN

AW77	5.00	BIRD GAME
AW78	75.00	BIG GAME

1968 NON-RESIDENT CANADIAN & ALIEN

AW79	25.00	SPRING BEAR
AW80	50.00	SPECIAL BIG GAME
AW81	15.00	WHITETAIL DEER

1968 NON-RESIDENT ALIEN

AW82	25.00	BIRD GAME, deep coral & red
AW83	150.00	BIG GAME, salmon

1968 SPECIAL LICENSE

AW84	7.50	ANTELOPE, white, black
AW85	5.00	ELK (S416-S418)
AW86	5.00	WAINWRIGHT DEER
AW87	5.00	NON-TROPHY SHEEP
AW88	1.00	SAGE GROUSE

1969 RESIDENT

Dimensions & perfs. same as 1968

AW89	2.50	BIRD GAME, grey, scarlet
AW90	5.00	SPRING BEAR
AW91	7.50	GRIZZLY BEAR
AW92	7.50	CARIBOU, yellow, red
AW93	3.00	MULE DEER, yellow, brown
AW94	3.00	WHITETAIL DEER, pink, red
AW95	5.00	ELK, pink, green
AW96	7.50	GOAT
AW97	5.00	MOOSE, pink, blue
AW98	5.00	ZONE 1 MOOSE
AW99	7.50	TROPHY SHEEP, pale blue, dark blue

	Face Value	Description
AW100	2.00	DUPLICATE LICENSE
AW101	7.50	SPECIAL ANTELOPE

1969 NON-RESIDENT CANADIAN

AW102	5.00	BIRD GAME
AW103	75.00	BIG GAME

1969 NON-RESIDENT CANADIAN & ALIEN

AW104	50.00	SPECIAL BIG GAME
AW105	25.00	SPRING BEAR
AW106	15.00	WHITETAIL DEER

1969 NON-RESIDENT ALIEN

AW107	25.00	BIRD GAME
AW108	150.00	BIG GAME, pale brown & dark brown

1970 RESIDENT.

Year imprinted on stamp.
Perf. 12½. Size: 31 x 39 mm
Forest scene background. All are yellow-brown with black lettering. Some non-resident stamps larger size.

AW109	2.50	BIRD GAME
AW110	10.00	BIG GAME M.E.D.
AW111	5.00	BLACK BEAR
AW112	10.00	GRIZZLY BEAR
AW113	10.00	CARIBOU
AW114	5.00	MULE DEER
AW115	3.00	WHITETAIL DEER
AW116	5.00	ELK
AW117	5.00	MOOSE
AW118	5.00	ZONE 1 MOOSE
AW119	10.00	TROPHY SHEEP
AW120	2.00	DUPLICATE LICENSE
AW121	3.00	ARCHERY

1970 NON-RESIDENT CANADIAN

AW122	5.00	BIRD GAME
AW123	75.00	SPECIAL BIG GAME

1970 NON-RESIDENT ALIEN

AW124	50.00	BIRD GAME

1970 NON-RESIDENT CANADIAN & ALIEN

AW125	25.00	BLACK BEAR
AW126	25.00	BLACK BEAR ZONE 1
AW127	200.00	GRIZZLY BEAR
AW128	100.00	CARIBOU
AW129	50.00	MULE DEER
AW130	50.00	WHITETAIL DEER
AW131	100.00	ELK
AW132	100.00	MOOSE
AW133	50.00	MOOSE ZONE 1
AW134	200.00	TROPHY SHEEP

1970 SPECIAL LICENSE

AW135	10.00	ANTELOPE
AW136	5.00	WAINWRIGHT DEER
AW137	5.00	ELK (S416-418)
AW138	5.00	NON-TROPHY SHEEP

1971 RESIDENT

Same design as 1970, but blue on white

AW139	2.50	BIRD GAME
AW140	10.00	BIG GAME M.E.D.
AW141	5.00	BLACK BEAR
AW142	10.00	GRIZZLY BEAR
AW143	10.00	CARIBOU
AW144	25.00	COUGAR
AW145	5.00	MULE DEER
AW146	3.00	WHITETAIL DEER
AW147	5.00	ELK
AW148	5.00	MOOSE
AW149	10.00	TROPHY SHEEP

Face Value		Description
AW150	2.00	DUPLICATE LICENSE
AW151	3.00	ARCHERY

1971 NON-RESIDENT CANADIAN
AW152	5.00	BIRD GAME, rose, blue
AW153	75.00	SPECIAL BIG GAME

1971 NON-RESIDENT CANADIAN & ALIEN
AW154	25.00	BLACK BEAR
AW155	200.00	GRIZZLY BEAR
AW156	100.00	CARIBOU
AW157	50.00	MULE DEER
AW158	50.00	WHITETAIL DEER
AW159	100.00	ELK
AW160	100.00	MOOSE
AW161	50.00	ZONE 1 MOOSE
AW162	200.00	TROPHY SHEEP

1971 NON-RESIDENT ALIEN
AW163	50.00	BIRD GAME, blue, red

1971 SPECIAL LICENSE
AW164	10.00	ANTELOPE
AW165	5.00	WAINWRIGHT DEER
AW166	5.00	NON-TROPHY SHEEP

1972 RESIDENT
Same design. Brown on white.

AW167	2.50	BIRD GAME
AW168	5.00	BLACK BEAR
AW169	10.00	GRIZZLY BEAR
AW170	10.00	CARIBOU
AW171	10.00	COUGAR
AW172	5.00	MULE DEER
AW173	3.00	WHITETAIL DEER
AW174	5.00	ELK
AW175	5.00	MOOSE
AW176	10.00	TROPHY SHEEP
AW177	2.00	DUPLICATE LICENSE
AW178	3.00	ARCHERY

1972 NON-RESIDENT CANADIAN & ALIEN
AW179	5.00	BIRD GAME
AW180	25.00	BLACK BEAR
AW181	200.00	GRIZZLY BEAR
AW182	100.00	CARIBOU
AW183	75.00	COUGAR
AW184	50.00	MULE DEER
AW185	50.00	WHITETAIL DEER
AW186	100.00	ELK
AW187	100.00	MOOSE
AW188	200.00	TROPHY SHEEP

1972 NON-RESIDENT CANADIAN
AW189	5.00	BIRD GAME
AW190	75.00	SPECIAL BIG GAME

1972 NON-RESIDENT ALIEN
AW191	50.00	BIRD GAME

1972 SPECIAL LICENSE
AW192	10.00	ANTELOPE
AW193	5.00	WAINWRIGHT DEER
AW194	5.00	ELK (S416-418)
AW195	10.00	GOAT
AW196	5.00	NON-TROPHY SHEEP

1973 RESIDENT
New format.

Perf. 12½. Size: 59 x 34 mm

Alpine scene background.

Green letters on yellow brown background.

AW197	2.50	BIRD GAME
AW198	5.00	BLACK BEAR
AW199	10.00	GRIZZLY BEAR
AW200	10.00	CARIBOU

Face Value		Description
AW201	10.00	COUGAR
AW202	5.00	MULE DEER
AW203	3.00	WHITETAIL DEER
AW204	5.00	ELK
AW205	5.00	MOOSE
AW206	10.00	TROPHY SHEEP
AW207	2.00	DUPLICATE
AW208	3.00	ARCHERY

1973 NON-RESIDENT CANADIAN & ALIEN
AW209	25.00	BLACK BEAR
AW210	200.00	GRIZZLY BEAR
AW211	100.00	CARIBOU
AW212	75.00	COUGAR
AW213	50.00	MULE DEER
AW214	50.00	WHITETAIL DEER
AW215	100.00	ELK
AW216	150.00	MOOSE
AW217	100.00	MOOSE ZONE 1
AW218	200.00	TROPHY SHEEP

1973 NON-RESIDENT CANADIAN
AW219	5.00	BIRD GAME
AW220	75.00	SPECIAL BIG GAME

1973 NON-RESIDENT ALIEN
AW221	50.00	BIRD GAME

1973 SPECIAL LICENSE
AW222	10.00	ANTELOPE
AW223	5.00	WAINWRIGHT DEER
AW224	5.00	ELK (S416-S418)
AW225	10.00	GOAT
AW226	5.00	NON-TROPHY SHEEP

1974 RESIDENT
Mountain scene background. Coral pink, letters in purple

AW227	2.50	BIRD GAME
AW228	5.00	BLACK BEAR
AW229	10.00	GRIZZLY BEAR
AW230	10.00	CARIBOU
AW231	10.00	COUGAR
AW232	6.00	MULE DEER
AW233	3.00	WHITETAIL DEER
AW234	5.00	ELK
AW235	5.00	MOOSE
AW236	5.00	ZONE 1 MOOSE
AW237	10.00	TROPHY SHEEP
AW238	2.00	DUPLICATE LICENSE
AW239	3.00	ARCHERY

1974 NON-RESIDENT CANADIAN & ALIEN
AW240	25.00	BLACK BEAR
AW241	200.00	GRIZZLY BEAR
AW242	100.00	CARIBOU
AW243	75.00	COUGAR
AW244	50.00	MULE DEER
AW245	50.00	WHITETAIL DEER
AW246	100.00	ELK
AW247	150.00	MOOSE
AW248	100.00	ZONE 1 MOOSE

1974 NON-RESIDENT CANADIAN
AW249	5.00	BIRD GAME
AW250	75.00	SPECIAL BIG GAME

1974 NON-RESIDENT ALIEN
AW251	50.00	BIRD GAME

1974 SPECIAL LICENSE
AW252	10.00	ANTELOPE
AW253	5.00	WAINWRIGHT DEER
AW254	5.00	ELK (S416-S418)
AW255	5.00	ANTLERLESS ELK

Face Value		Description
AW256	10.00	GOAT
AW257	5.00	NON-TROPHY SHEEP

1975 RESIDENT
Similar to 1974, greenish yellow with brown lettering.
Size 34 x 60 mm

AW258	2.50	BIRD GAME
AW259	5.00	BLACK BEAR
AW260	10.00	GRIZZLY BEAR
AW261	10.00	CARIBOU
AW262	10.00	COUGAR
AW263	5.00	MULE DEER
AW264	3.00	WHITETAIL DEER
AW265	5.00	ELK
AW266	5.00	ZONE 1 MOOSE
AW267	5.00	MOOSE
AW268	10.00	TROPHY SHEEP
AW269	2.00	DUPLICATE
AW270	3.00	ARCHERY

1975 NON-RESIDENT CANADIAN & ALIEN

AW271	25.00	ANTELOPE
AW272	25.00	BLACK BEAR
AW273	200.00	GRIZZLY BEAR
AW274	100.00	CARIBOU
AW275	75.00	COUGAR
AW276	50.00	MULE DEER
AW277	50.00	WHITETAIL DEER
AW278	100.00	ELK
AW279	200.00	MALE MOOSE
AW280	100.00	ZONE 1 MOOSE

1075 NON-RESIENT CANADIAN

AW281	5.00	BIRD GAME
AW282	75.00	SPECIAL BIG GAME

1975 NON-RESIDENT ALIEN

AW283	50.00	BIRD GAME

1975 SPECIAL LICENSE

AW284	10.00	ANTELOPE
AW285	5.00	WAINWRIGHT DEER
AW286	5.00	ANTLERLESS ELK
AW287	5.00	ELK (S416-418)
AW288	10.00	GOAT
AW289	5.00	NON-TROPHY SHEEP

1976 RESIDENT
Game animals as background. salmon, dark brown letters.
Size 29 x 60 mm

AW290	2.50	BIRD GAME
AW291	5.00	BLACK BEAR
AW292	10.00	GRIZZLY BEAR
AW293	10.00	CARIBOU (MALE)
AW294	10.00	COUGAR
AW295	5.00	MULE DEER
AW296	3.00	WHITETAIL DEER
AW297	5.00	ELK
AW298	5.00	MOOSE
AW299	5.00	ZONE 1 MOOSE
AW300	10.00	TROPHY SHEEP
AW301	2.00	DUPLICATE
AW302	3.00	ARCHERY

1976 NON-RESIDENT CANADIAN & ALIEN

AW303	25.00	ANTELOPE
AW304	25.00	BLACK BEAR
AW305	200.00	GRIZZLY BEAR
AW306	100.00	CARIBOU
AW307	75.00	COUGAR
AW308	50.00	MULE DEER
AW309	50.00	WHITETAIL DEER

1976 NON-RESIDENT CANADIAN

AW310	5.00	BIRD GAME
AW311	75.00	SPECIAL BIG GAME
AW312	50.00	BIRD GAME

1976 SPECIAL LICENSE

AW313	10.00	ANTELOPE
AW314	5.00	WAINWRIGHT DEER
AW315	5.00	ELK (S416-S418)
AW316	10.00	GOAT
AW317	5.00	MOOSE, CYPRESS HILL
AW318	5.00	NON-TROPHY SHEEP

1977 RESIDENT
Year on stamp. Background: whitetailed deer in blue on
white, dark blue lettering

AW319	2.50	BIRD GAME
AW320	5.00	BLACK BEAR
AW321	10.00	GRIZZLY BEAR
AW322	10.00	CARIBOU
AW323	10.00	COUGAR
AW324	5.00	MULE DEER
AW325	3.00	WHITETAIL DEER
AW326	5.00	ELK (MALE)
AW327	5.00	MOOSE
AW328	5.00	ZONE 1 MOOSE
AW329	10.00	TROPHY SHEEP
AW330	2.00	DUPLICATE
AW331	3.00	ARCHERY

1977 NON-RESIDENT

AW332	25.00	BLACK BEAR
AW333	200.00	GRIZZLY BEAR
AW334	100.00	CARIBOU
AW335	75.00	COUGAR
AW336	50.00	MULE DEER (MALE)
AW337	50.00	WHITETAIL DEER
AW338	100.00	ELK
AW339	200.00	MOOSE
AW340	200.00	ZONE 1 MOOSE
AW341	200.00	TROPHY SHEEP
AW342	25.00	WOLF

1977 NON-RESIDENT CANADIAN

AW343	25.00	ANTELOPE
AW344	5.00	BIRD GAME
AW345	75.00	SPECIAL BIG GAME

1977 NON-RESIDENT ALIEN

AW346	50.00	BIRD GAME

1977 SPECIAL LICENSE

AW347	10.00	ANTELOPE
AW348	10.00	NON-TROPHY ANTELOPE
AW349	5.00	WAINWRIGHT DEER
AW350	5.00	ANTLERLESS MULE DEER
AW351	4.00	ANTLERLESS WHITETAIL DEER
AW352	5.00	ANTLERLESS ELK
AW353	5.00	ELK (S416-S418)
AW354	10.00	GOAT
AW355	5.00	NON-TROPHY SHEEP

1978 RESIDENT
Year on stamps.
Background: male mule deer in yellowish buff, dark brown
letters. Size 29 x 60 mm

AW356	2.50	BIRD GAME
AW357	5.00	BLACK BEAR
AW358	10.00	GRIZZLY BEAR
AW359	10.00	CARIBOU
AW360	10.00	COUGAR
AW361	5.00	MULE DEER
AW362	5.00	WHITETAIL DEER
AW363	5.00	ELK

Face Value		Description
AW364	5.00	MOOSE
AW365	20.00	TROPHY SHEEP
AW366	2.00	DUPLICATE
AW367	3.00	BOWHUNTING

1978 NON-RESIDENT

AW368	25.00	ANTELOPE
AW369	25.00	BLACK BEAR
AW370	200.00	GRIZZLY BEAR
AW371	100.00	CARIBOU
AW372	75.00	COUGAR
AW373	50.00	MULE DEER
AW374	50.00	WHITETAIL DEER
AW375	100.00	ELK
AW376	100.00	MOOSE
AW377	100.00	ZONE 1 MOOSE

1978 NON-RESIDENT CANADIAN

AW378	5.00	BIRD GAME
AW379	75.00	SPECIAL BIG GAME

1978 NON-RESIDENT ALIEN

AW380	50.00	BIRD GAME

1978 SPECIAL LICENSE

AW381	10.00	TROPHY ANTELOPE
AW382	10.00	WAINWRIGHT DEER
AW383	5.00	ANTLERLESS MULE DEER
AW384	5.00	ANTLERLESS WHITETAIL DEER
AW385	5.00	ANTLERLESS ELK
AW386	10.00	CYPRESS HILLS ELK
AW387	10.00	CYPRESS HILLS MOOSE
AW388	10.00	GOAT
AW389	5.00	NON-TROPHY SHEEP

1979 RESIDENT

Year on stamp
Background: elk in dark grey on grey. dark green lettering

AW390	5.00	BIRD GAME
AW391	5.00	BLACK BEAR
AW392	10.00	GRIZZLY BEAR
AW393	10.00	CARIBOU
AW394	10.00	COUGAR
AW395	5.00	MULE DEER
AW396	5.00	WHITETAIL DEER
AW397	5.00	ELK
AW398	5.00	MOOSE
AW399	10.00	TROPHY SHEEP
AW400	2.00	DUPLICATE
AW401	5.00	BOW HUNTNG

1979 SPECIAL LICENSE

AW402	10.00	TROPHY ANTELOPE
AW403	10.00	WAINWRIGHT DEER
AW404	5.00	ANTLERLESS MULE DEER
AW405	5.00	ANTLERLESS WHITETAIL DEER
AW406	5.00	ANTLERLESS ELK
AW407	10.00	CYPRESS HILLS ELK
AW408	10.00	GOAT
AW409	5.00	NON-TROPHY SHEEP

1979 NON-RESIDENT CANADIAN

AW410	5.00	BIRD GAME
AW411	25.00	TROPHY ANTELOPE

1979 NON-RESIDENT CANADIAN & ALIEN

Dark yellow on yellow, dark blue letters

AW412	5.00	BIRD GAME
AW413	25.00	BLACK BEAR
AW414	200.00	GRIZZLY BEAR
AW415	100.00	CARIBOU
AW416	75.00	COUGAR
AW417	50.00	MALE MULE DEER
AW418	50.00	MALE WHITETAIL DEER
AW419	100.00	MALE ELK

Face Value		Description
AW420	100.00	ZONE 1 MALE MOOSE
AW421	200.00	TROPHY SHEEP
AW422	25.00	WOLF
AW423	10.00	BOW HUNTING

1979 NON-RESIDENT ALIEN

AW424	50.00	BIRD GAME

1980 RESIDENT

Year on stamps.
Background: alpine scene blue, lettering dark blue

AW425	5.00	BIRD GAME
AW426	10.00	BLACK BEAR
AW427	20.00	GRIZZLY BEAR
AW428	20.00	CARIBOU
AW429	20.00	COUGAR
AW430	10.00	GENERAL MULE DEER
AW431	10.00	GENERAL WHITETAIL DEER
AW432	10.00	GENERAL ELK
AW433	10.00	GENERAL MOOSE
AW434	20.00	TROPHY SHEEP
AW435	2.00	DUPLICATE
AW436	5.00	BOW HUNTING

1980 SPECIAL LICENSE

AW437	20.00	TROPHY ANTELOPE
AW438	10.00	NON-TROPHY ANTELOPE
AW439	20.00	WAINWRIGHT DEER
AW440	20.00	CYPRESS HILLS ELK
AW441	20.00	GOAT
AW442	10.00	NON-TROPHY SHEEP

1980 NON-RESIDENT CANADIAN

AW443	125.00	TROPHY ANTELOPE
AW444	5.00	BIRD GAME
AW445	50.00	BLACK BEAR
AW446	125.00	GRIZZLY BEAR
AW447	100.00	CARIBOU
AW448	100.00	COUGAR
AW449	75.00	MALE MULE DEER
AW450	75.00	MALE WHITETAIL DEER
AW451	100.00	MALE ELK
AW452	100.00	MALE MOOSE
AW453	200.00	TROPHY SHEEP
AW454	75.00	WOLF

1980 NON-RESIDENT ALIEN

AW455	50.00	BIRD GAME
AW456	100.00	BLACK BEAR
AW457	250.00	GRIZZLY BEAR
AW458	200.00	CARIBOU
AW459	150.00	MALE MULE DEER
AW460	150.00	MALE WHITETAIL DEER
AW461	200.00	MALE ELK
AW462	200.00	MALE MOOSE
AW463	100.00	ZONE 1 MALE MOOSE
AW464	200.00	TROPHY SHEEP
AW465	150.00	WOLF

1981 RESIDENT

Year on stamps. Blue mountain scene, black lettering

AW466	5.00	BIRD GAME
AW467	10.00	BLACK BEAR
AW468	20.00	GRIZZLY BEAR
AW469	20.00	COUGAR
AW470	10.00	GENERAL MULE DEER
AW471	10.00	GENERAL WHITETAIL DEER
AW472	10.00	GENERAL ELK
AW473	10.00	GENERAL MOOSE
AW474	20.00	TROPHY SHEEP
AW475	2.00	DUPLICATE
AW476	5.00	BOW HUNTING
AW477	20.00	TROPHY ANTELOPE
AW478	10.00	NON-TROPHY ANTELOPE

Face Value		Description
AW479	20.00	WAINWRIGHT DEER
AW480	20.00	CYPRESS HILLS ELK
AW481	20.00	MOUNTAIN GOAT
AW482	10.00	NON-TROPHY SHEEP

1981 NON-RESIDENT CANADIAN

AW483	125.00	TROPHY ANTELOPE
AW484	5.00	BIRD GAME
AW485	50.00	BLACK BEAR
AW486	125.00	GRIZLLY BEAR
AW487	100.00	COUGAR
AW488	75.00	GENERAL MALE MULE DEER
AW489	75.00	GENERAL WHITETAIL DEER
AW490	100.00	GENERAL ELK
AW491	100.00	GENERAL MOOSE
AW492	125.00	TROPHY SHEEP
AW493	10.00	BOW HUNTING

1981 NON-RESIDENT ALIEN

AW494	50.00	BIRD GAME
AW495	100.00	BLACK BEAR
AW496	250.00	GRIZZLY BEAR
AW497	200.00	COUGAR
AW498	150.00	MALE MULE DEER
AW499	150.00	MALE WHITETAIL DEER
AW500	200.00	MALE ELK
AW501	200.00	MALE MOOSE
AW502	150.00	ZONE 1 MALE MOOSE
AW503	250.00	TROPHY SHEEP
AW504	150.00	WOLF
AW505	15.00	BOW HUNTING

1982 RESIDENT

Background: bull elk. Pinkish buff with darker design.
Other printing in black.

AW506	5.00	BIRD GAME
AW507	10.00	BLACK BEAR
AW508	20.00	GRIZZLY BEAR
AW509	20.00	COUGAR
AW510	10.00	GENERAL MULE DEER
AW511	10.00	GENERAL WHITETAIL DEER
AW512	10.00	GENERAL ELK
AW513	10.00	GENERAL MOOSE

1982 RESIDENT SPECIAL LICENSES

AW514	20.00	TROPHY SHEEP
AW515	2.00	DUPLICATE LICENSE
AW516	5.00	BOW HUNTING
AW517	20.00	TROPHY ANTELOPE
AW518	10.00	NON-TROPHY ANTELOPE
AW519	20.00	CAMP WAINWRIGHT DEER
AW520	20.00	CYPRESS HILLS ELK
AW521	20.00	WMU F-300 ELK
AW522	20.00	MOUNTAIN GOAT
AW523	10.00	NON-TROPHY SHEEP

1982 NON-RESIDENT CANADIAN

AW524	25.00	BIRD GAME
AW525	50.00	BLACK BEAR
AW526	125.00	GRIZZLY BEAR
AW527	100.00	COUGAR
AW528	75.00	MALE MULE DEER
AW529	75.00	MAIL WHITE-TAILED DEER
AW530	100.00	MALE ELK
AW531	100.00	MALE MOOSE
AW532	125.00	TROPHY SHEEP
AW533	75.00	WOLF
AW534	10.00	BOW HUNTING

1982 SPECIAL LICENSE

AW535	125.00	TROPHY ANTELOPE

1982 NON-RESIDENT ALIEN

AW536	100.00	BLACK BEAR

Face Value		Description
AW537	250.00	GRIZZLY BEAR
AW538	200.00	COUGAR
AW539	150.00	MALE MULE DEER
AW540	150.00	MALE WHITE-TAILED DEER
AW541	200.00	MALE ELK
AW542	200.00	MALE MOOSE
AW543	100.00	MALE MOOSE ZONE 1
AW544	250.00	TROPHY SHEEP
AW545	150.00	WOLF
AW546	15.00	BOW HUNTING

1983 RESIDENT

Background: grizzly bear - dark green on pale green

AW547	5.00	BIRD GAME
AW548	10.00	BLACK BEAR
AW549	20.00	GRIZZLY BEAR
AW550	20.00	COUGAR
AW551	10.00	GENERAL MULE DEER
AW552	10.00	GENERAL WHITE-TAILED DEER
AW553	10.00	GENERAL ELK
AW554	10.00	GENERAL MOOSE
AW555	20.00	TROPHY SHEEP
AW556	2.00	DUPLICATE LICENSE
AW557	5.00	BOWHUNTING

1983 RESIDENT SPECIAL LICENSES

AW558	20.00	TROPHY ANTELOPE
AW559	10.00	NON-TROPHY ANTELOPE
AW560	20.00	CAMP WAINWRIGHT DEER
AW561	20.00	CYPRESS HILLS ELK
AW562	20.00	MOUNTAIN GOAT
AW563	10.00	NON-TROPHY SHEEP
AW564	20.00	WMU F-300 ELK

1983 NON-RESIDENT CANADIAN

Grizzly bear design in yellow

AW565	25.00	BIRD GAME
AW566	50.00	BLACK BEAR
AW567	125.00	GRIZZLY BEAR
AW568	100.00	COUGAR
AW569	75.00	MALE MULE DEER
AW570	75.00	MALE WHITE-TAILED DEER
AW571	100.00	MALE ELK
AW572	100.00	MALE MOOSE
AW573	125.00	TROPHY SHEEP
AW574	15.00	WOLF
AW575	10.00	BOW HUNTING

1983 SPECIAL LICENSE

AW576	125.00	TROPHY ANTELOPE

1983 NON-RESIDENT ALIEN

AW577	50.00	BIRD GAME
AW578	100.00	BLACK BEAR
AW579	250.00	GRIZZLY BEAR
AW580	200.00	COUGAR
AW581	150.00	MALE MULE DEER
AW582	150.00	MALE WHITE-TAILED DEER
AW583	200.00	MALE ELK
AW584	200.00	MALE MOOSE
AW585	100.00	MALE MOOSE ZONE 1
AW586	25.00	WOLF
AW587	15.00	BOW HUNTING

1984 RESIDENT

Background: black bear - dark rust on pale rust

AW588	5.00	BIRD GAME
AW589	10.00	BLACK BEAR
AW590	20.00	GRIZZLY BEAR
AW591	20.00	COUGAR
AW592	10.00	GENERAL MULE DEER
AW593	10.00	GENERAL WHITE-TAILED DEER
AW594	10.00	GENERAL ELK
AW595	10.00	GENERAL MOOSE

Face Value		Description
AW596	20.00	TROPHY SHEEP
AW597	10.00	QUOTA LICENSE
AW598	2.00	DUPLICATE LICENSE
AW599	5.00	BOW HUNTING

1984 RESIDENT SPECIAL LICENSES

AW600	20.00	TROPHY ANTELOPE
AW601	10.00	NON-TROPHY ANTELOPE
AW602	20.00	CAMP WAINWRIGHT DEER
AW603	20.00	CYPRESS HILLS ELK
AW604	20.00	MOUNTAIN GOAT
AW605	10.00	NON-TROPHY SHEEP

1984 NON-RESIDENT CANADIAN
Black bear design - puple on pale purple

AW606	25.00	BIRD GAME
AW607	50.00	BLACK BEAR
AW608	125.00	GRIZZLY BEAR
AW609	100.00	COUGAR
AW610	75.00	MALE MULE DEER
AW611	75.00	MALE WHITE-TAILED DEER
AW612	100.00	MALE ELK
AW613	100.00	MALE MOOSE
AW614	100.00	TROPHY SHEEP
AW615	25.00	WOLF
AW616	10.00	BOW HUNTING

1984 SPECIAL LICENSE

AW617	125.00	TROPHY ANTELOPE

1984 NON-RESIDENT ALIEN

AW618	50.00	BIRD GAME
AW619	100.00	BLACK BEAR
AW620	250.00	GRIZZLY BEAR
AW621	200.00	COUGAR
AW622	150.00	MALE MULE DEER
AW623	150.00	MALE WHITE-TAILED DEER
AW624	200.00	MALE ELK
AW625	200.00	MALE MOOSE
AW626	100.00	MALE MOOSE ZONE 1
AW627	250.00	TROPHY SHEEP
AW628	25.00	WOLF
AW629	15.00	BOW HUNTING

1985 RESIDENT
Background: mountain goat - dark green on pale green

AW630	5.00	GAME BIRD
AW631	10.00	BLACK BEAR
AW632	20.00	GRIZZLY BEAR
AW633	20.00	COUGAR
AW634	10.00	GENERAL MULE DEER
AW635	10.00	GENERAL WHITE-TAILED DEER
AW636	10.00	GENERAL ELK
AW637	10.00	GENERAL MOOSE
AW638	20.00	NORTHERN ANTLERLESS MOOSE
AW639	20.00	TROPHY SHEEP
AW640	—	PHEASANT
AW641	10.00	QUOTA LICENSE
AW642	2.00	DUPLICATE LICENSE
AW643	5.00	BOW HUNTING

1985 RESIDENT SPECIAL LICENSES

AW644	20.00	TROPHY ANTELOPE
AW645	10.00	NON-TROPHY ANTELOPE
AW646	20.00	CAMP WAINWRIGHT DEER
AW647	20.00	CYPRESS HILLS ELK
AW648	10.00	ANTLERLESS ELK
AW649	10.00	ANTLERLESS MULE DEER
AW650	20.00	MOUNTAIN GOAT
AW651	10.00	NON-TROPHY SHEEP
AW652	10.00	PHEASANT
AW653	25.00	GAME BIRD
AW654	50.00	BLACK BEAR
AW655	125.00	GRIZZLY BEAR

Face Value		Description
AW656	100.00	COUGAR
AW657	75.00	GENERAL MULE DEER
AW658	75.00	GENERAL WHITE-TAILED DEER
AW659	100.00	GENERAL ELK
AW660	100.00	GENERAL MOOSE
AW661	250.00	TROPHY SHEEP
AW662	15.00	WOLF
AW663	10.00	PHEASANT
AW664	10.00	BOW HUNTING

1985 SPECIAL LICENSE

AW665	125.00	TROPHY ANTELOPE

1985 NON-RESIDENT ALIEN

AW666	50.00	GAME BIRD
AW667	100.00	BLACK BEAR
AW668	250.00	GRIZZLY BEAR
AW669	200.00	COUGAR
AW670	150.00	GENERAL MULE DEER
AW671	150.00	GENERAL WHITE-TAILED DEER
AW672	200.00	GENERAL ELK
AW673	200.00	GENERAL MOOSE
AW674	100.00	MALE MOOSE ZONE 1
AW675	250.00	TROPHY SHEEP
AW676	25.00	WOLF
AW677	10.00	PHEASANT
AW678	15.00	BOW HUNTING

1986 RESIDENT
Design: Buck and Doe Mule deer; grey on grey

AW679	5.00	GAME BIRD
AW680	10.00	BLACK BEAR
AW681	20.00	GRIZZLY BEAR
AW682	20.00	COUGAR
AW683	10.00	GENERAL MULE DEER
AW684	10.00	GENERAL WHITE-TAILED DEER
AW685	10.00	GENERAL ELK
AW686	10.00	GENERAL MOOSE
AW687	20.00	NORTHERN ANTLERLESS MOOSE
AW688	20.00	TROPHY SHEEP
AW689	5.00	ANTLERLESS DEER WMU212,248
AW690	10.00	STRATHCONA WHITE-TAILED DEER
AW691	10.00	PHEASANT
AW692	10.00	QUOTA
AW693	5.00	BOW HUNTING

1986 SPECIAL LICENSES

AW694	20.00	TROPHY ANTELOPE
AW695	10.00	NON-TROPHY ANTELOPE
AW696	20.00	CAMP WAINWRIGHT DEER
AW697	20.00	CYPRESS HILLS ELK
AW698	10.00	ANTLERLESS MULE DEER
AW699	10.00	ELK WMU 243
AW700	10.00	ELK WMU 300
AW701	10.00	BLACK DIAMOND ELK
AW702	20.00	MOUNTAIN GOAT
AW703	10.00	ANTLERLESS ELK
AW704	10.00	NON-TROPHY SHEEP

1986 NON-RESIDENT CANADIAN

AW705	25.00	GAME BIRD
AW706	50.00	BLACK BEAR
AW707	125.00	GRIZZLY BEAR
AW708	100.00	COUGAR
AW709	75.00	GENERAL MULE DEER
AW710	75.00	GENERAL WHITE-TAILED DEER
AW711	100.00	GENERAL ELK
AW712	100.00	GENERAL MOOSE
AW713	250.00	TROPHY SHEEP
AW714	15.00	WOLF
AW715	10.00	PHEASANT
AW716	10.00	BOW HUNTING

Face Value		Description

1986 SPECIAL LICENSE

AW717	125.00	TROPHY ANTELOPE

1986 NON-RESIDENT ALIEN

AW718	50.00	GAME BIRD
AW719	100.00	BLACK BEAR
AW720	250.00	GRIZZLY BEAR
AW721	200.00	COUGAR
AW722	150.00	GENERAL MULE DEER
AW723	150.00	GENERAL WHITE-TAILED DEER
AW724	200.00	GENERAL ELK
AW725	200.00	GENERAL MOOSE
AW726	100.00	ANTLERED MOOSE ZONE 1 & 16
AW727	250.00	TROPHY SHEEP
AW728	25.00	WOLF
AW729	10.00	PHEASANT
AW730	15.00	BOW HUNTING

1987 RESIDENT

Design: circular 1987 Wildlife seal, green on green. Special licenses now converted to computer generated tags.

AW731	6.00	GAME BIRD
AW732	20.00	BLACK BEAR
AW733	40.00	GRIZZLY BEAR
AW734	40.00	COUGAR
AW735	10.00	MULE DEER
AW736	10.00	WHITE-TAILED DEER
AW737	15.00	ELK
AW738	11.00	MOOSE
AW739	40.00	TROPHY SHEEP
AW740	5.00	ANTLERLESS DEER WMU 212 & 248
AW741	10.00	STRATHCONA WHITE-TAILED DEER
AW742	10.00	PHEASANT
AW743	3.00	DUPLICATE LICENSE
AW744	5.00	BOW HUNTING

1987 NON-RESIDENT CANADIAN

Lavender on lavender

AW745	—	GAME BIRD
AW746	100.00	BLACK BEAR
AW747	138.00	GRIZZLY BEAR
AW748	110.00	COUGAR
AW749	83.00	MULE DEER
AW750	83.00	WHITE-TAILED DEER
AW751	110.00	ELK
AW752	110.00	MOOSE
AW753	275.00	TROPHY SHEEP
AW754	15.00	PHEASANT
AW755	11.00	BOW HUNTING

1987 SPECIAL NON-RESIDENT

AW756	138.00	TROPHY ANTELOPE

1987 NON-RESIDENT ALIEN

AW757	22.00	GAME BIRD
AW758	150.00	BLACK BEAR
AW759	275.00	GRIZZLY BEAR

Face Value		Description
AW760	220.00	COUGAR
AW761	165.00	MULE DEER
AW762	165.00	WHITE-TAILED DEER
AW763	220.00	ELK
AW764	220.00	MOOSE
AW765	275.00	TROPHY SHEEP
AW766	110.00	ANTLERED MOOSE ZONES 1 & 16
AW767	15.00	PHEASANT
AW768	17.00	BOW HUNTING

1988 RESIDENT

Background: a bull elk bugling, blue design on white stamp.

AW769	6.00	GAME BIRD
AW770	10.00	FALL BLACK BEAR
AW771	10.00	SPRING BLACK BEAR
AW772	5.00	COUGAR
AW773	10.00	MULE DEER
AW774	10.00	WHITE-TAILED DEER
AW775	15.00	ELK
AW776	11.00	MOOSE
AW777	40.00	TROPHY SHEEP
AW778	10.00	PHEASANT
AW779	5.00	ANTLERLESS DEER WMU 212, 248
AW780	22.00	NORTHERN ANTLERLESS MOOSE
AW781	10.00	STRATHCONA WHITE-TAILED DEER

1988 NON-RESIDENT CANADIAN

Design in buff on white.

AW782	—	GAME BIRD
AW783	50.00	FALL BLACK BEAR
AW784	50.00	SPRING BLACK BEAR
AW785	110.00	COUGAR
AW786	83.00	MULE DEER
AW787	83.00	WHITE-TAILED DEER
AW788	110.00	ELK, background in 3 colours
AW789	110.00	MOOSE
AW790	275.00	TROPHY SHEEP
AW791	11.00	BOW HUNTING
AW792	15.00	PHEASANT

1988 NON-RESIDENT ALIEN

AW793	50.00	GAME BIRD
AW794	75.00	FALL BLACK BEAR
AW795	75.00	SPRING BLACK BEAR
AW796	220.00	COUGAR
AW797	165.00	MULE DEER
AW798	165.00	WHITE-TAILED DEER
AW799	220.00	ELK
AW800	220.00	MOOSE
AW801	275.00	TROPHY SHEEP
AW802	110.00	ANTLERED MOOSE ZONES 1 & 16
AW803	15.00	PHEASANT
AW804	17.00	BOW HUNTING

ALBERTA RESOURCE DEVELOPMENT STAMPS

In 1973, Alberta began issuing a wildlife resource development stamp which was required to be purchased by everyone buying a hunting license. The 1973 stamp is an adhesive. From 1985 on the stamps come as an adhesive and as an imprinted stamp on the huntine license.

AWR1	1.00	1973	perf. 12.5, buff, green lettering.
AWR2	1.00	1974	printed on page 3 of license, pink, green lettering
AWR3	2.00	1975	printed on page 3 of license, pink, green lettering
AWR4	2.00	1976	printed page 3 of license, pink, blue lettering
AWR5	2.00	1977	printed on page 3 of license, pink, brown lettering
AWR6	2.00	1978	printed on back of page 5, pink, brown lettering
AWR7	2.00	1979	printed on back of page 5, grey, green lettering
AWR8	2.00	1980	printed on back of page 5, blue, dark blue lettering
AWR9	5.00	1981	printed on back of page 5, grey, black lettering
AWR10	5.00	1982	ELK: brown, white lettering, back of page 5
AWR11	5.00	1983	GRIZZLY: brown, blue lettering, back of page 5
AWR12	5.00	1984	BEAR: black, brown lettering, back of page 5
AWR13	5.00	1985	GOAT: green, black lettering, front of page 5, red number
AWR14	5.00	1985	ADHESIVE STAMP: 60 x 24 mm, green on green, p. 12.5
AWR15	5.00	1986	DEER: rose lilac, black letters, front page 5, red number
AWR16	5.00	1986	ADHESIVE STAMP: rouletted, grey
AWR17	6.00	1987	WILDLIFE EMBLEM: green, black letters, front page 5, red number
AWR18	6.00	1987	ADHESIVE STAMP: perf. 12.2, pale blue green
AWR19	6.00	1988	MOOSE: blue, black lettering, front of page 5, red number
AWR20	6.00	1988	ADHESIVE STAMP: perf. 12.7, pale blue

HUNTING LICENSE STAMPS

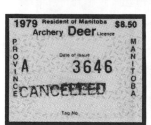

BRITISH COLUMBIA HUNTING LICENSE STAMPS

			Uncan.	Used
1982 Deer Hunting				
Adhesive, size 23 x 27 mm				
BCHL1	$8	green, no value on stamp	—	—
BCHL2	$8	red	—	—
1983-1986 Deer Hunting				
Size 28 x 25 mm				
BCHL3	$8	license, black on white	—	—
BCHL4	$8	red on grey	—	—
BCHL5	$8	stamp, black on pink	—	—
1984 Extra License				
Size 26 mm x 30 mm				
BCHL6	$8	stamp, black on white	—	—
BCHL7	$8	mp., black on orange red	—	—

			Uncan.	Used
1987-1989 New System Introduced				
Size 46 mm x 16 mm				
Hunting license and a series of species licenses. The fee for each species license differs and is not shown on the stamp.				
BCHL8	—	red	—	—
BCHL9	—	brown	—	—
BCHL10	—	green	—	—
BCHL11	—	green	—	—
BCHL12	—	blue	—	—
BCHL13	—	orange	—	—
BCHL14	—	purple	—	—
BCHL15	—	diagonal green stripes	—	—
BCHL16	—	diagonal blue stripes	—	—
BCHL17	—	diagonal orange stripes	—	—
BCHL18	—	diagonal red stripes	—	—
BCHL19	—	diagonal purple stripes	—	—

HUNTING STAMPS
Manitoba, North West Territories and Saskatchewan have also issued hunting stamps. Much work has already been done and complete listings should be available for the next edition of this catalogue.

Also recently issued are the BC fishing stamps, federal fishing stamps for use in BC, and possibly others. We will list these once complete details are available.

100 DIFFERENT
CANADA & PROVINCES REVENUES

A great starter selection with a wonderful range of issues right back to 1868.
High catalogue value and good value for only $25.00

SPECTACULAR
1883, 1897 TOBACCO STAMP
COLLECTION

Beautifully engraved large size tobacco stamps, some more than 100 years old. Each is like a work of art, displaying a workmanship no longer seen. This wonderful group of 16 different can be yours for only $175.00.

The above is only a tiny sampling of the wonderful revenue material available.

We regularly publish our fully illustrated newsletter *"ReveNews"™* which you'll find filled with special offers, unusual items, rarities and all kinds of material to enhance your revenue collection.

Three or four times each year we hold revenue stamp auctions. Our catalogues are lavishly illustrated and feature an incredible range of revenue material, as well as semi-official airmails, cinderellas, Telephone & Telegraph franks, Tobacco stamps and other related material. Foreign revenues are frequently offered as well.

Comprehensive Canadian revenue price lists are issued on a regular basis. You'll find something for every collection.

ASK FOR FREE SAMPLE & SUBSCRIPTION INFORMATION

Naturally, everything we sell is sold with the following guarantee:
SATISFACTION GUARANTEED OR MONEY BACK

E.S.J. van Dam Ltd.

P.O. Box 300, Bridgenorth, Ontario, Canada K0L 1H0
Phone (705) 292-7013   Fax: (705) 292-6311
Revenue Stamps Bought & Sold.

CANADA REVENUE METERS

This fascinating revenue meter material has been around for about 50 years.

Although millions must have been used, only large users used them. They seem to be quite hard to find and research by various specialists has turned up only a limited amount of material.

METERS USED BY:

Private Users
Companies in the private sector such as Tuckett, Quaker Oats, Canada Life Assurance, Dunlop, and others used them on cheques, sight drafts and other financial instruments to pay excise tax. These are no longer in use, and are quite scarce now.

British Columbia Government
Used in place of Law Stamps, which are slowly being phased out. Currently in use in most B.C. courts, these meters are still common.

Unemployment Insurance Commission

Large users of UIC stamps used meters. These are no longer in use.

Quebec Government
These were used in place of Law Stamps, and are currently still in use.

Below are some sample illustrations of the various types of meters, many others exist. Please contact the author regarding revenue meters in your possession and we will publish a complete listing in a furure edition of this catalogue.

NEW WESTMINSTER

REGISTRY

PALAIS DE JUSTICE

SOREL

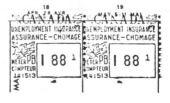

The 1991 SCOTT Specialized Catalogue of Canadian Stamps

Perfect Bound $11.95

Spiral Bound $13.95

SCOTT

Specialized Catalogue of Canadian Stamps

Including:
New Brunswick, Nova Scotia,
Prince Edward Island,
British Columbia and Vancouver Island,
Newfoundland

BIGGER AND BETTER THAN EVER!

- The 1991 editions have been expanded to 352 pages
- English and French editions are available in perfect bound or spiral bound formats
- Many new listings including Newfoundland Plate and Inscription Blocks, expanded Plate Proof and Trial Colour listings for Canadian and colonial stamps, Wildlife Habitat Conservation stamps, and more.
- Many additional variety listings

Available from your favourite dealer or book store, or order from the publisher:

UNITRADE ASSOCIATES
91 TYCOS DRIVE, TORONTO, ONTARIO M6B 1W3
TEL: (416) 787-5658   FAX: (416) 787-7104

UNI-SAFE

Orders to the publisher should include $2.00 postage & handling
plus all applicable sales taxes.

The following pages list SOME of the philatelic literature carried by UNITRADE ASSOCIATES

All titles can be obtained through your favourite dealer – or order from Unitrade at the address shown following this list.

PHILATELIC LITERATURE – CANADA

THE STANDARD CATALOGUE OF CANADIAN BOOKLET STAMPS
SECOND EDITION *By Bill McCann*

The most complete source of information on Canadian Booklets and Booklet Panes, this book lists values for complete booklets, mint and used booklet panes for Canada and Newfoundland. Includes listings for all major and most minor varieties, printing quantities and other statistics.

6"x9", 72 pages, saddle stitched, illustrated $5.95

SPECIALIZED CATALOGUE OF CANADA POST OFFICIAL FIRST DAY COVERS
FIRST EDITION *By Marcel Cool*

Fully illustrated in colour, this catalogue lists all Canada Post Official First Day Covers from their inception in 1971 to date. Prices are given for singles, pairs, blocks of four and plate blocks on cover. Combination covers are also listed and priced. The popular Scott Numbering System is used throughout and most varieties found on covers are also listed for each category.

6"x9", 56 pages, saddle stitched, colour illustrated $7.95

THE STANDARD CANADA PRECANCEL CATALOGUE
FIRST EDITION *Edited by H.G. Walburn*
(with J.E. Kraemer and Hans Reiche)

This is the first major work on Canadian Precancels in many years and the most complete available. All known varieties of Canadian precancels are priced and listed by type – bar precancels, town and city precancels, and precancels with perforated initials. All Town and City precancels are conveniently catalogued alphabetically within each province.

6"x9", 56 pages, saddle stitched, illustrated $6.95

CANADIAN STAMPS WITH PERFORATED INITIALS
FOURTH EDITION *By Johnson & Tomasson*

A completely revised edition of this popular work. This is a fully illustrated catalogue of all known Canadian "Perfins" with much new material added. A rarity factor is given for each item listed.

6"x9", 120 pages, perfect bound, BNAPS Perfin Study Group $9.95

CANADIAN PICTURE POST CARD CATALOGUE – 1988
FIRST EDITION *By Wally Gutsman*

This work is the first ever listing and catalogue of Canadian Post Cards. All known Canadian Picture Post Cards are catalogued and priced according to Post Card Era. Well illustrated, this is an excellent guide for anyone interested in the post cards of Canada.

6"x9", 80 pages, perfect bound, illustrated $9.95

WEBB POSTAL STATIONERY CATALOGUE OF CANADA AND NEWFOUNDLAND
FIFTH EDITION *Edited by Earle Covert & Bill Walton*

This completely revised and reset, this definitive catalogue and price guide includes all the known varieties of postal stationery from Canada and Newfound. Sections include Envelopes, Post Bands and Wrappers, Letter Sheets, Aerogrammes, Letter Cards, Post Cards, Official Pictorial Cards, Essays and Proofs, and much more.

6"x9", 136 pages, perfect bound, illustrated $14.95

CANADIAN STAMP HANDBOOKS
Edited by Michael Milos

This is a new concept in Canadian philatelic handbooks. To be published over the next few years and distributed by The Unitrade Press, this is a series of priced, loose-leaf handbooks prepared by specialists for the specialist collector. These handbooks will provide, when completed, a valuable, comprehensive work which can be updated quickly and economically as new information or new conditions occur. See your local dealter or write The Unitrade Press for information.

Now Available:

No. 1 THE FIRST CENTS ISSUE $2.95
No. 2 THE CENTENNIAL ISSUE $5.95
No. 3 THE EDWARD VII ISSUE $2.95
No. 4 THE ADMIRAL ISSUE $3.95
No. 5 CANADIAN CELLO PAQS & SOUVENIR ARTICLES $3.95
No. 6 THE SMALL QUEENS $3.95
No. 7 CARICATURES & LANDSCAPES $6.95
No. 8 THE MEDALLION ISSUE $6.95

Arnell—STEAM AND THE NORTH ATLANTIC MAILS

The history of postal communication between England and her North American colonies during the period of transition from sail to steam. Profusely illustrated with covers from the period, this well-researched volume is a must for anyone interested in covers from the pre-postage stamp era. Also an excellent history of the development of steam transport on the North Atlantic, outlining the development of the Cunard Lines.

6"x9", 295 pages, hard cover, illustrated $75.00

Bailey and Toop—CANADIAN MILITARY POST OFFICES TO 1986

This handbook and checklist is an update and expansion of "Canadian Military Postmarks" published in 1978. Illustrated with hammer strikes from as early as 1886 to the present day, it catalogues all Canadian Military Post Offices progressively by campain or era of involvement. Wherever possible, the actual opening and closing dates for each post office are listed. Post offices for all three military services are included, as well as those for Prisoner of War internment camps during both World Wars and the Canada Militia from 1909 on. A checklist for all listings is included.

6"x9", 96 pages, perfect bound, illustrated $14.95

Eckhardt—THE MYSTERY OF THE PRINCE EDWARD QUEEN

The interesting story of how Allen Taylor produced a fictitious 10 cent PEI stamp that completely fooled the philatelic world in 1872.

16 pages, saddle stitched, illustrated $2.95

Gutzman—THE CANADIAN PATRIOTIC POST CARD HANDBOOK 1904-1914

This handbook lists the known Canadian Patriotic Postcards by publisher. Includes an illustrated listing of address sides. A rarity factor pricing guide is incorporated for all cards listed.

6"x9", 144 pages, perfect bound, illustrated $12.95

Kell—THE POSTAL HISTORY OF THE DISTRICT OF ASSINIBOIA 1882-1905

Includes background history, population, the system of the townships, development of the railways and the early mail routes. The cancellations are described and classified. Each post office is listed alphabetically giving its location, background, opening and closing dates, name changes, serial number, postmasters, cancellers, earliest and latest dates, handstamps and general interest.

6"x9", 192pages, perfect bound, illustrated $19.95

Lehr—THE POSTAGE STAMPS AND CANCELLATIONS OF PRINCE EDWARD ISLAND

This excellent reference offers much new information on the postage stamps of P.E.I. Includes chapters on Proofs and Essays, Secondary Dies, Fakes and Forgeries. The second part of the book covers the cancellations used by the P.E.I. post offices.

6"x9", 174 pages, hard cover, illustrated $39.95

MacDonald—THE NOVA SCOTIA POST: IT'S OFFICES, MASTERS AND MARKS 1700-1867
The definitive work on the subject covering the colonial period to Confederation. Includes full-sized illustrations of all markings.
6"x9", 300 pages, hard cover, illustrated $29.95

Marler—CANADA: THE ADMIRAL ISSUE 1911-1925
New printing of this popular work covering Marler's Notes on the 1911-1925 issue. Covers coils, booklets, guidelines and dots, etc.
6"x9", 80 pages, perfect bound, illustrated $10.00

Newman—THE BICKERDIKE MACHINE PAPERS
Anyone interested in early machine cancels will be familiar with the name "Bickerdike", though few will be able to explain it. This book covers the development and use of the Bickerdike machine for cancellations. Research for the book uncovered the personal note book of one of the original owners of the Bickerdike patents, shedding great light on the heretofore foggy history of the Bickerdike machine.
6"x9", 144 pages, perfect bound, illustrated $24.95

O'Reilly—NORTHWEST TERRITORIES POSTAL CANCELLATIONS 1907-1986
This work consists primarily of a detailed listing (with illustrations) of the postal markings used in the N.W.T. in this period. Each post office is listed alphabetically giving its location, background, opening and closing dates, name changes, etc. Special features include detailed listing on the Eastern Arctic Patrol (including the ship itineries) and the United States Army Post Offices located in the N.W.T.
8½"x11", 230 pages, perfect bound, illustrated $24.95

Reiche—ADMIRAL CANCELS
An interesting pamphlet on the various types of cancels used during the period.
5½"x8½", 20 pages, saddle stitched $2.95

Reiche—Canada Constant Precancel Varieties
6"x9", 48 pages, saddle stitched, illustrated $7.95

Reiche—THE CANADIAN LATHEWORK DESIGN
Illustrated 12 page pamphlet $2.50

Reiche—CANADA STEEL ENGRAVED CONSTANT PLATE VARIETIES
Rarity factor provided for all known plate varieties.
6"x9", 118 pages, perfect bound, illustrated $14.95

Reiche—CONSTANT PLATE VARIETIES OF THE CANADIAN SMALL QUEENS
Up-dated information, now the definitive work.   144 pages soft cover ... $5.50

Reiche & Chung—THE CANADIAN POSTAGE DUE STAMPS
A detailed research in two sections. The first covers the actual stamps—the second an in-depth look at the treating and rating of unpaid, shortpaid, redirected and undeliverable mail. Well illustrated.
6"x9", 72 pages, perfect bound, illustrated $9.95

Sessions—THE EARLY RAPID CANCELLING MACHINES OF CANADA
This original work reviews the history and development of Rapid Cancelling machines in Canada. Covers period of use, types of cancellations, time marks, varieties, chronology and obliterating dies. Rarity factors have been applied to each item classified.
144 pages, perfect bound, illustrated $17.95

Shantz & Demaray—THE POST OFFICES AND POSTMARKS OF LONDON, ONTARIO
An interesting booklet covering the postal history of this Ontario city. Illustrated listing of postmarks used.   24 pages solft cover $2.95

Robert C. Smith—Ontario Post Offices
A two-volume set, Volume I is an alphabetical listing of the 8090 post offices in Ontario, past and present,

indicating opening and closing dates, city, township and alternate names. The companion Volume II is a listing by country and district. An absolute must for Ontario postal historians.

Volume I - An Alphabetical Listing 6"x9", 216 pages, spiral bound $35.95
Volume II - By County and District 6"x9", 262 pages, spiral bound $45.95
Two Volume Set $71.95

Steinhart—CIVIL CENSORSHIP IN CANADA DURING WORLD WAR I
A new study by Canada's leading postal historian, this is a well- illustrated documentation of the censorship of the Canadian mails during the First World War.
77 pages $12.95

H.G. Walburn et al.—THE CANADA PRECANCEL HANDBOOK
A logical companion to the Standard Canada Precancel Catalogue, the handbook delves into the identification of all known varieties of precancels. Well illustrated and cross-referenced by precancels and stamp issues overprinted.
6"x9", 184 pages, perfect bound, illustrated $16.95

1984 CANADA METER & PERMIT POSTAGE STAMPS SPECIALIZED CATALOGUE
Including Revenues, House of Commons, etc. $10.00

THE POSTAGE STAMPS OF NEW BRUNSWICK AND NOVA SCOTIA *(Argenti)*
Detailed study including die and plate proofs, postal rates, usage of the stamps, forgeries, appendixes.
8½"x11", 272 pages, illustrated, hard bound (Reprint) $39.95

THE POSTAGE STAMPS AND POSTAL HISTORY OF CANADA *(Boggs)*
The "Bible" of Canadian philately. Absolutely essential for background data not found elsewhere. This classic includes the design, paper and plate makeup of the stamps, postal stationery, and cancels.
912 pages, illustrated, hard cover. (Reprint) $65.00

THE POSTAGE STAMPS AND POSTAL HISTORY OF NEWFOUNDLAND *(Boggs)*
Including early postal history, the samps from 1857 to 1942, airmails and their overprints, postage due, postal stationery, cancellations and postmarks. Listings of the post offices to 1940.
256 pages, illustrated, hard cover (Reprint) $35.00

SUPPLEMENT TO THE TOBACCO TAX PAID STAMPS OF CANADA AND NEWFOUNDLAND INCLUDING A STUDY OF THE LIQUOR BOTTLE SEALS OF CANADA *(Brandom)*
Lists and prices these Canadian revenues.
BNAPS, 8½"x11", 106 pages, illustrated, ... $10.95

CANADA POST OFFICES 1755-1895 *(Campbell)*
Exhaustive listong of the postmarks used during this period. Including opening and closing dates.
8½"x11", 218 pages, hard cover, illustrated $40.00

CANADIAN FANCY CANCELLATIONS OF THE 19TH CENTURY *(Day and Smythies)*
BNAPS, 158 pages, perfect bound, illustrated,, ... $9.95

THE COLONIAL POSTAL SYSTEMS AND POSTAGE STAMPS OF VANCOUVER ISLAND AND BRITISH COLUMBIA 1849-1871 *(Deaville)*
A tremendous work—The authoritative study of this area.
211 pages, 14 plates, hard cover, (Reprint) $39.95

CANADIAN MAIL BY RAIL 1836-1867 *(Gillam)*
168 pages, illustrated., hard bound $32.95

LA PREMIERE ROUTE POSTAL AU CANADA 1763- 1851 *(Des Rivieres)*
Covers the lst Canadian postal route from Quebec City to Montreal. Including postal rates, cancellations and postal history.
French text, 43 pages, illustrated, ... $4.95

THE SQUARED CIRCLE POSTMARKS OF CANADA *(Dr. Moffatt and Glen Hansen)*
Exhaustive detail and illustrations including rarity factors and actual market values.
BNAPS. 485 pages, illustrated, hard cover $40.00

UPPER AND LOWER CANADA CROSS-BORDER MAIL TO 1851 *(Palmer)*
.... $23.00

CANADA: THE 1967-1973 DEFINITIVE ISSUE *(Irwin & Murray Freedman)*
(Original authors Keene & Hughes) Extensively revised (1984) 2nd edition. Well researched and easy-to-follow. Including new section on perfins and postal rates.
8½"x11", 112 pages, illustrated, ... $17.95

STAMPS OF BRITISH NORTH AMERICA *(Jarrett)*
Ranked as one of the most comprehensive and exhaustive works ever published on Canadian philately, it contains essential background information and extensive treatment of postmarks and cancellations. The work also covers revenues, postal stationery, wrappers, bisects and counterfeits.
Reprint, 624 pages, illustrated, hard cover $45.00

THE SEMI-OFFICIAL AIR STAMPS OF CANADA 1924-1934 *(Longworth-Dames)*
Complete background, all known cachets, flight information, cover quantities, study of the stamps, etc.
5¾"x8¼", 120 pages, perfect bound, illustrated. $9.95

CATALOGUE OF CANADIAN RAILWAY CANCELLATIONS AND RELATED TRANSPORTATION POSTMARKS *(Ludlow & Shaw)*
Lists the cancellation, period used, type of cancel, rarity factor, and statistical data.
8½"x11", 272 pages, illustrated, spiral bound, ... $34.95

CANADIAN PRECANCELLED POSTAL STATIONERY HANDBOOK *(Marley)*
Covers Envelopes, Post Bands and Post Cards. Including illustrated flaps, precancel types, the town numerals, etc.
52 pages, illustrated, perfect bound $12.00

THE NEWFOUNDLAND POST OFFICE MAIL ASSORTING OFFICE, NORTH SYDNEY, NOVA SCOTIA, 1906-1949 *(McGuire)*
Monograph of the movement of mail between Newfoundland and Canada prior to Confederation.
11 pages, illustrated,, perfect bound $1.50

THE CANADIAN OCEAN MAIL CLERK 1860-1887 *(MacKenzie)*
National Postal Museum, 48 pages, illustrated, perfect bound $2.50

Canadian Philatelic Handbook *(Mechem)*
Many interesting facts of postal history.
38 pages, illustrated, perfect bound $3.95

Fakes and Forgeries of New Brunswick & Prince Edward Island (Mitchell)
Including list of forgers, specific issues, bisects and faked cancellations, die and plate proofs.
43 pages, illustrated, perfect bound $4.95

THE POST OFFICE OF VAUGHAN TOWNSHIP, ONTARIO *(O'Rourke)*
Interesting study of history of the Post Offices of this Township which will give the reader an inside view of Rural Post Office development and management. Including opening and closing dates, postmasters, location, regulations, etc.
8½"x11", 140 pages., illustrated, perfect bound $19.95

CANADA: B.N.A. PHILATELY (AN OUTLINE) *(Richardson)*
A fascinating book, intended for the collector who has always collected by "Scott". This book was intended to introduce collectors to the great, wide, wonderful world of BNA Philately—including chapters on stampless covers, cancellations, precancels, perfins, postal stationery, covers, revenues, and much more! Also extensive bibliography.
64 pages, illustrated, ... $9.95

THE POSTAL HISTORY OF THE CANADIAN CONTINGENTS IN THE ANGLO-BOER WAR 1899-1902 *(Rowe)*

Background information. Covers the lst, wnd and 3rd Contingents, the South African Constabulary and the Royal Tour of 1901. Including the postal corps, nursing service, Y.M.C.A., contingent/regimental stationary, Canadian postage used in South Africa, postmarks, bibliography and a Rarity Scale.

104 pages, illustrated, hard cover $35.00

THE POSTAL HISTORY OF THE POST CARD IN CANADA 1871-1911 *(Steinhart)*

Traces the history of the postal stationery card, private post card pictorial view card from their first use in Canada in 1871 through to 1911, the end of the Edwardian Era. Mainly postal history including postal regulations and rates..

65 pages, illustrated, perfect bound $9.95

THE CANADA POSTAL ACT AND POST OFFICES 1878 AND THE CANADA SPLIT RING PROOFS *(Symonds)*

Much useful information to postal historians not found anywhere but in the original Post Office records.

138 pages, illustrated, spiral bound, ... $19.95

CANADA: THE WAR TAX STAMPS *(War Tax Study Group)*

A well researched study on another area of the Admiral era. Very specialized with many illustrations.

36 pages, illustrated, ... $4.95

HISTORY OF RURAL MAIL IN CANADA *(Wilcox)*

Reissue of the original 1918 book with new illustrations, introduction, table of contents and index.

74 pages, illustrated, ... $2.50

THE POSTAL HISTORY OF YUKON TERRITORY, CANADA *(Woodall)*

Covers the establishment of the Postal Service in the Yukon. Including dog sled, steamer, RCMP patrol, railroads, aircraft and private express companies to carry the mail. Postmasters, opening and closing dates and name changes for all post offices. Postal markings.

272 pages, illustrated, hard cover $38.95

OTHER PHILATELIC REFERENCES

THE STAMP BUG *(Douglas and Mary Patrick)*

EXCELLENT! One of the best handbooks of stamp collecting ever published in Canada. The Stamp Bug is an illustrated introduction to stamp collecting for young readers. Features: how to obtain, sort and mount stamps; postmarks and perforations; organizing a stamp club, etc.

96 pages, illustrated, perfect bound $7.50

BROOKMAN STAMP PRICES

U.S., U.N. and Canada – Spiral 1991 Edition $12.95
U.S., U.N. and Canada – Bound 1991 Edition $8.95
U.S. First Day Covers & Postal Collectibles – Spiral 1991 Edition ......$ 12.95

SEVEN SEAS AUSTRALIAN STAMP CATALOGUE

20TH EDITION Pocket $8.95

Brookman—STAMP COLLECTING IS FUN $8.95

Scott—1991 U.S. POCKET STAMP CATALOGUE & CHECKLIST $10.95

Harris—1990-1991 FALL/WINTER CATALOGUE (US, UN, Canada) $8.95

Order all of the above titles from your favourite dealer, or direct from:

UNITRADE ASSOCIATES
91 TYCOS DRIVE, TORONTO, ONTARIO   M6B 1W3
TEL: (416) 787-5658   FAX: (416) 787-7104
UNI-SAFE   Orders to Unitrade must include $2 postage and handling.

Write for a complete catalogue of Unitrade philatelic products, free on request.